How to Create a
Successful
Children's
Picture Book

Best-selling author Bobbie Hinman tells you how she
created, self-published and sold over **50,000** copies
of her award-winning children's picture books

BOBBIE HINMAN

Bestfairybooks.com

How to Create a Successful Children's Picture Book
Copyright © 2017 Bobbie Hinman
Cover design and page layout: Jeff Urbancic

ISBN: 978-0-9786791-9-4
Library of Congress Control Number: 2015934992

Publisher's Cataloging-in-Publication
(Provided by Quality Books, Inc.)

    Hinman, Bobbie, author.
       How to create a successful children's picture book / Bobbie Hinman.
       pages cm
       Includes bibliographical references and index.
       LCCN 2015934992

       ISBN 978-0-9786791-9-4
       1. Picture books for children--Authorship.
      2. Picture books for children--Technique. 3. Picture books
      for children--Marketing.   I. Title.

      PN147.5.H56 2017   808.06'8
                     QBI16-900073

Best Fairy Books
www.bestfairybooks.com

In loving memory of my Mom and Dad.
My passion for reading began as I sat on their laps
and they let me turn the pages.

And to the owner of the fortune cookie factory
who kept me on task with these messages:

"You can find magic
wherever you look.
Sit back and relax,
all you need is a book."

— Dr. Seuss

Table of Contents

Remember: Every Good Story Needs a
Beginning, a Middle and an End

Part 1.
The Beginning:
An Idea Takes Shape

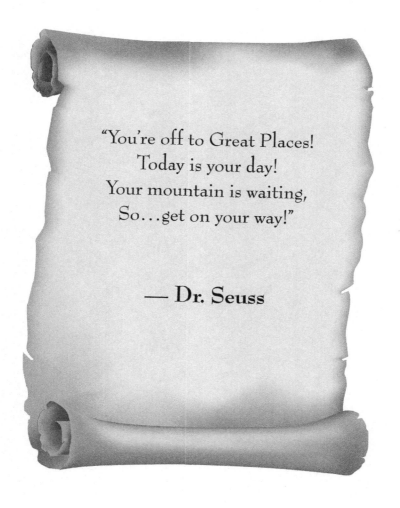

"You're off to Great Places!
Today is your day!
Your mountain is waiting,
So...get on your way!"

— Dr. Seuss

Introduction

I will always be thankful for the awards my books have won and the smiles my books have brought to thousands of children all over the world. I have sold over 50,000 copies of my fairy books by doing everything in this book, and I will tell you exactly what I did to accomplish this feat. I'm not going to suggest that you do anything I haven't done—and am still doing. Your personal goal may be to reach a large audience, or perhaps you simply want to see your name in print. You may want to build your own warehouse and fill it with books, or maybe you just want to print enough books for your family and friends. Whichever path you choose, I am here to help guide you.

You may decide not to do everything I did, and that's fine; it's all up to you. Feel free to pick and choose whatever best fits your needs. Before you begin, ask yourself three questions: How badly do I want this? How hard am I willing to work? What is my budget?

There are many how-to-publish books on the market, and they aim to tell you everything you need to know to write and market your book. But too often something is missing: This business is not just about the books. This business is about people—the people who help you write the book, the people who buy your book, the people you meet at schools, bookstores and festivals, and most of all, the very young people who will read your book. Unless you are a complete Jack-of-all-trades, if you want a great book, you will need help along the way. You will need an editor, an illustrator, a printer, and so many others. What you also need to know is that people, mainly the very young ones, will be your greatest assets. That's why, when people ask me if I self-published my books, my answer is usually, "No, I could never do it all myself." Follow me as I show you how I solved the problems of self-publishing. Pay special attention to the people who helped me, from the early input of my focus groups to the happy little munchkins reading my books tonight in their beds. This book is as much about them as it is about me. Every one of these people left their mark on my business. I wouldn't be where I am without them.

How Long Will it Take to Become an Overnight Success?

When people tell me how "lucky" I am that my books have received so much attention, I just smile and tell them that "the harder I work, the luckier I seem to be." I hope all of the talented, budding writers who may be looking for a "lucky break" will realize that the hard work has to come first. It's a wonderful feeling to be noticed in a vast sea of books, but first you have to row the boat.

Warning: Stamina Required!

If you want to take the ride, you will also need to work hard and take risks. I will show you how these risks can be minimized if you make your product as close to "perfect" as possible. Remember: Your book will only be as good as you make it. Find the best people to help you, and then go do it!

Welcome to the world of publishing. Hold on—this will be an exciting ride!

People Who Will Help You Do It *Yourself*

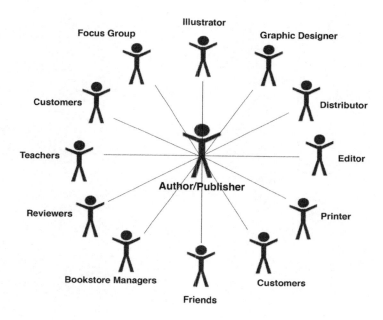

1. How My Story Begins

Every good story has a beginning, a middle and an end. This is *my* **beginning:**

How was I to know that simply by combing my grand-daughter's hair, I was standing on the threshold of a new career? It all started when my husband and I were babysitting our six-year-old twin granddaughters, Emily and Lindsay, and their nine-year-old brother, Justin. It was actually day two of our "ten-days-that-seemed-like-an-eternity" babysitting stint, but that's another story!

I was trying to comb through Emily's morning tangles; however, she was wailing loudly, and well, you know the scene. So...I did what grandmas do so well: I made up a story. Suddenly, out of nowhere, came the story of the sweet little Knot Fairy who visits sleeping children and loves to tangle their hair. Emily stopped crying. She loved the story and begged me to tell it every day, not only to her, but to her brother and sister and all of their friends. Not only one time, but over and over...

To make a very long story very short, I was energized by my grandkids' excitement. Deep down, I had always known I wanted to write a children's book. Hubby and I were both retired. So, why not? We could do this! We could publish it ourselves! My use of exclamation marks is to indicate how much we believed in ourselves from the start. This is key. If you think you will fail, you probably will. The secret is to plan to succeed. We created our own publishing company: We incorporated, hired the best illustrator we could find, hired a talented graphic designer, found the perfect printer, and Best Fairy Books, Inc. was born. This year we published our 5th children's picture book. Our books have received 25 children's book awards, and we have sold over 50,000 copies. I am told that's a pretty good track record.

Our grandkids have all been a part of the process. They were the source of the first idea (tangled hair) and of many new ideas; they are my biggest fans and my best, and most honest, critics. Their names appear on all of my books' dedication pages, and their precious little voices are featured on the CDs that accompany my books.

I realize now that my grandkids changed my life in ways I never could have imagined. Their enthusiasm is contagious; they have learned, as I have, to always be open to new possibilities and to go after whatever life has to offer—even in the Golden Years!

I am not an overnight success; however, I *am* a success. And you can be, too! My goal is to make it easier for you by sharing everything I have learned along the way. While many people choose traditional publishing, I chose to form my own company. I wanted to control every aspect of the creation and produce the best books possible. Whichever way you choose, I hope my hints for writing and marketing your books will make success easier for *you* to accomplish.

Good luck and happy travels!

2. Becoming Successful as a Self-Publisher

"What do you mean you're going to start a publishing company? You can't do that!"

That's what I heard when I announced to my friends and family that I was going into the publishing business. Little did they know that, although I was a card-carrying member of AARP, there was no cap on my ideas, creativity or drive. The truth is that my years of life experience had finally given me the knowledge (and admittedly, the guts) to do something I had always wanted to do. As the author and co-author of seven traditionally published cookbooks, I pretty much thought I knew everything there was to know about the book business (big gulp here!). As it turned out, the information I *didn't* know could fill volumes. Thankfully, I *did* know that, no matter who publishes your book, you, the author, must plan to promote, promote, promote. Oh, and did I say promote?

I could have submitted my ideas to other publishers. It worked with my cookbooks. However, the publishing world today is more competitive than ever, especially when it comes to children's books. I didn't want to start sending query letters and possibly fill a shoebox with rejection notices while waiting for the right publisher to show interest in my book. This time I wanted to be the one to make the decisions about when the book would be published, what the cover would look like, which illustrator to hire and all the other migraine-producing challenges. And when it came to promoting my books, even working with a large publishing company, I spent many hours working hard to supplement their marketing efforts.

Yes, there are drawbacks to doing it all yourself. Laying out the money is scary, but doing that gave me further incentive to work hard and produce a good book. I felt I had to be willing to invest in myself. And then there's the time factor. There's no getting around it; writing and publishing a book takes a lot of time. For me, marketing still remains the hardest part of the process. For the first 4 years, I made it my goal to work on promotion several hours a day, at least 5 days a week. Are you willing to do this—and more? Fortunately, I have a tremendous amount of help from my husband and business partner, Harry. If you are also blessed to have someone who shares the drive and passion for your business, you are very lucky.

Would I recommend self-publishing? Yes, if you do it right. Let's face it: As self-publishers, our books are often judged more critically and held to a higher standard than traditionally published books. Therefore, if we're going to represent ourselves, let's make our books the very best. There's no room in today's market for more run-of-the-mill books. Competition is tougher than it has ever been. On my journey I have verified an important fact that some self-publishers fail to recognize: In order to compete in the book world, you MUST produce a high-quality product!

This is a good time to sit down and have a talk with yourself. Ask yourself why you want to write a book. If it's to make a "fast buck" or gain fame and fortune, you might not want to quit your day job just yet. Being realistic, even if your book is wildly successful, it will be a minimum of a few years, and take mountains of marketing, before you reap the financial rewards you may be seeking.

Maybe you are writing because you have a message to share with the world, or you want to produce an entertaining book, or maybe you just love to write. Whatever the reason, before you start, you need to set your own personal goals. Take a hard look at the time factor. Will you be able to find the time to write? How about the discipline? If you have a full-time job, how will you fit everything into your life without putting too much pressure on yourself and those around you? These are all things to consider. Writing is a difficult process and if you take the hit-or-miss approach, there's a good chance the quality will suffer.

Can you do it?

My message is a resounding "YES, YOU CAN!" followed by a very stern "IF YOU DO IT RIGHT!" followed by a sincere "HOW BADLY DO YOU WANT IT?"

In order to compete, you MUST produce a high-quality book!

3. Traditional Publishing vs. Self-Publishing

As a first step, it's important to understand the different types of publishing formats available to writers today. No longer is there just one path to publishing. As a result, writers often find themselves in a quandary, wondering which way to turn. Whether you are seeking the traditional publishing experience or want to carve your own path, the choice is completely within your grasp.

Having had experience with both traditional *and* self-publishing, I would like to draw a few comparisons between the two. In my early cookbook career, my books were published by a traditional publisher. One important thing I learned from this experience is that writing a book is not about sitting back and collecting royalties. It didn't take me long to realize that if my books were going to be successful, I would have to step into the arena of marketing and promotion. Any marketing efforts that I added to the publisher's agenda was at my own expense. I traveled all over the country as a featured speaker and guest on radio and TV shows (even the Regis Philbin Show). I visited schools, hospitals, bookstores, and basically any place an event could be arranged. Funny thing—every time I had a successful event, I sold more books! It works! Knowing that I would be taking on many promotional tasks anyway, I was excited about the possibility of self-publishing my children's books. I knew I would be responsible for paying for and marketing the books myself. Was I up to the challenge? It seemed like an adventure waiting to happen, and I'm so glad I did it.

I'm sad to say that to many people "self publishing" means poorly edited books with skimpy illustrations, poor storylines and run-of-the mill covers. Unfortunately, there are too many self-published books that do fit this description. Here's the test: If you can look at a book and tell immediately that it was self-published, the writer didn't do everything possible to create and produce a more professional product. If you decide to self-publish, you must be willing to invest in producing a quality book, one that is properly conceived, written, edited and proofed, etc., and then promoted vigorously.

Before you make a final decision, here are a few basic comparisons to help you understand the differences between traditional publishing and self-publishing:

Traditional Publishing

Traditional publishing: You do not pay to publish your book. With traditional publishing, an author is offered a contract from a publisher to print, publish and sell his or her book through booksellers and other retailers, and to pay the author royalties from the sales. For the author, this involves first writing query letters to publishers and then sending manuscripts to any who show interest. An editor reads each manuscript and decides either to reject or publish the book. If accepted, the publisher puts up all the money to design, print and market the book, taking all the risk. The publisher also selects the illustrator and oversees the illustration process. With a legitimate traditional publisher, you will never be charged a fee to publish your book.

Self-Publishing

Self-publishing: *You* pay to publish your book. With self-publishing, the author basically becomes the publisher. The author/publisher must take responsibility for everything the traditional publisher does, including providing the funds necessary to hire the people required to do the job correctly. The author/publisher is responsible for overseeing book production, marketing and distribution, and implementing an advertising campaign.

A Few More Basic Differences

Costs:

With traditional publishing, you are almost always paid an advance. The amount can range from small sums to seven-digit figures (for the "big guns"). This is an advance against future sales, not a gift. You are also paid royalties on sales. You should not have to lay out any money. Important: If a publisher requires you to pay to have your book published, they are not really a traditional publisher. You are better off going to a Print on Demand (POD) publisher who lets you know up front that they are a printing service and are not pretending to be traditional publishers.

With self-publishing, your costs can run high. The costs vary, depending on a number of factors that I will talk about in later chapters. Just be aware that self-publishing authors pay for *everything*—design, editing, printing, advertising and distribution. Be sure you understand that with self-publishing, you can't make money without spending it. You will be undertaking a huge commitment and financial risk. Self-publishing works best for people who are good at budgeting their time and money—and are prepared to spend both.

So, which is more lucrative? Unless you sell tens of thousands of books with a traditional publisher, self-publishing can actually be more lucrative. You can set the price, and you don't have to share your profits. The downside is that you will need capital to get started. Still, if you hire the right people and market like crazy, this may be the most beneficial way to go.

Time frame:

With traditional publishing, it can take years for your idea to become a book. You may have to receive a shoebox-full of rejection letters before your book is accepted by a publisher. Large publishing houses can take months before even responding to your query letter. Even after being accepted, your book will have to wait its turn in the publisher's production schedule.

With self-publishing, an author can have a finished book within a short time period. How long is typical? I've met authors who have had their books completed in six months, but usually a part of the process will suffer if you try to rush it. Everyone involved needs time to do their part correctly, so be patient and do it right. My books have each taken a year for completion, *after* the story was written.

Marketing:

With traditional publishing, the publisher will do most of the marketing. I say "most" because the publisher has many books to promote, and yours may not always receive the individual attention you would like. You will need to step in and supplement the marketing, and the publisher will encourage you to do so.

With self-publishing, the author takes on full marketing responsibility. You will work very hard, but the money you make is all yours. See the last section of this book for lots of creative marketing tips.

Control:

Traditional publishers make all the decisions concerning your book. In most cases this is a good thing, but you will have to brace yourself and accept what they do, even if it is not what you had in mind.

With self-publishing, the author has all the control. You will oversee the content, design and appearance, as well as when and how the book is marketed and distributed.

Storage:

Traditional publishers store the books. They warehouse them and ship them to accounts as needed.

Self-publishers will have to secure safe storage for their books. Keep in mind that if you live in a warm climate, you should definitely consider climate-controlled storage for your books.

If you are planning to sign a contract with either a traditional, POD or hybrid publisher, be sure you know what your rights and responsibilities are before you sign.

4. Alternative Methods for Self-Publishing

Obviously, if you are reading this book, you are seriously interested in self-publishing. Before you get started, FYI...here's some information about other varieties of self-publishing available in today's market. You may have heard of some of these, and it's a good idea to understand what they represent. They are not publishing options that I chose; however, they may be right for you, and it's always beneficial to understand what else is out there.

Print on demand (POD). With POD, you pay a company to print your books in any quantity you wish, with no minimum required. POD companies offer printing and distribution services and do not pretend to be traditional publishers. You will pay a one-time setup fee, have control of your book's pricing and receive royalties as the books are sold. Unfortunately, the price can be extremely high, especially for very small quantities. POD companies will print for anyone willing to pay, which tends to lower the overall quality of the books. For the basic service, many of these companies do no editing or proofreading, and the books are often produced in paperback format with the least expensive materials. Everything else is considered an upgrade, with services such as editing or marketing offered at an additional cost. Sadly, in many cases the editing and marketing efforts are of poor quality.

I'm not trying to scare anyone; the news is not all bad. The advantages of POD are that there is no up-front outlay of capital, and you don't have to keep an inventory of books or fulfill orders. In most cases, the POD company handles all the sales, then sends the author a royalty, deducting the agreed-upon printing and distribution fees.

Subsidy publishing (or Vanity publishing). As with POD, the author pays for the printing of the book. Subsidy houses normally charge for their design, printing and distribution services, with their basic package often being of mediocre quality. Their distribution services are often scanty. As the books are sold, the author makes money from royalties. Basically, you will end up working as hard as if you self-published; however, you will only receive a royalty instead of the full amount of money your sales generate—and *you* will have paid for it all up front.

Hybrid publishing. This includes numerous variations on the different publishing methods. You really must do your homework and compare the differences. Each company has its own arrangements for printing, editing, marketing, royalties and fees. If *you* are paying, make sure you know what you are paying for.

Warning: More Pitfalls Ahead

There are a few more things to be aware of when deciding between the different types of self-publishing:

Beware of publishers who aren't really publishers. Be careful. Do your research and know who you are dealing with. There are many companies that call themselves "publishers" and do all sorts of things to entice novice authors. Most of these companies request an upfront free; others will claim they have no fees, yet later will charge you editorial or design fees. Some will require you to purchase a large quantity of your books at a ridiculously high price. I have even met authors who thought they were entering a contest and, after paying an entry, were later told they were winners and now qualified to buy multiple copies of their books if they published with that company. Also, beware of ads that promise to "get you published." Yes, they will publish your book—and *you* will pay for it.

Know who owns the ISBN and why it matters. Both traditional publishers and self-publishers own the ISBNs for the books they publish. The important thing to remember is that whoever owns the ISBN owns the rights to publish the book. If any printing company assigns an ISBN to your book, *they* own the publishing rights. If you use POD, be certain *you* own the ISBN and are only granting permission for the POD publisher to produce and distribute your book. Be keenly aware of what period of time is involved in this arrangement because the publishing rights should then revert back to you. Another issue: If a very large order comes their way, both traditional and self-publishers have the wiggle room to negotiate and make a deal, which is often necessary in any business. But what if a large order comes to the POD or subsidy publisher? The sad truth is that most are unwilling, or unable, to offer deep discounts; thus the sale is lost. I've heard a number of stories from authors who have experienced this, and there was nothing they could do about it. A few of these authors had no idea what an ISBN represents and were totally unaware of their lack of ownership. (Please read the information about ISBNs, what they are and how to obtain them, in the section titled "You Will Need to Apply for These...")

Know what your book should look like. This is so important! Of course you know what your book will look like, right? You know it will have a dragon on the cover and have lots of colorful characters. But do you know what belongs on the back cover and the spine? Do you have a Library of Congress number? If you are going to self-publish, whether with a POD company, a vanity press or on your own, *you* must be the one to make 100% sure that your book contains all the necessary components. Relying on a printing company to direct and inform you can have disastrous results. I have met authors who have poured their hard-earned dollars into books that were refused by major bookstores because there was no ISBN, or the book title was not on the spine, or the back cover was left completely blank—all because they were assuming the printer would guide them. Then there's the editing, and I can't say this enough: I implore you—whichever one of these paths you choose, please have your book professionally edited!

In Conclusion

Do your research! Before using POD or subsidy publishing companies, authors should definitely ask for samples of the companies' work and ask themselves if this is what they want their book to look like. They need to make sure to discuss the total price and know what to expect in the way of quality and service. The lines between self-publishing, POD and subsidy publishing have become increasingly blurred in the past few years, with new methods and companies appearing all the time. This is even more reason why research is so important.

If you plan to market your books to bookstores, and are using a POD company, ask the company for a list of books they have printed that are now in bookstores. You can then see for yourself the quality of their products. If they have no books to list, that will also tell you something.

If you sign a contract with either a POD or hybrid publisher, be sure you know what your rights and responsibilities are *before* you sign. Be sure there is a termination clause that allows you to withdraw from the book publishing arrangement, thereby reclaiming the rights to your book. And be sure there is a pro-vision in any contract allowing you to purchase books from the publisher at a discount. This will enable you to make a profit by selling these books to friends and relatives, as well as at book fairs and schools, and any other venue that is not in competition with your publisher's sales.

In my experience, the best way to create an outstanding picture book is to use high-quality offset printing. When ordering a large quantity (anything over 1,000 copies), offset printing through a private printing company has, for me, proven to be the best option.

Two POD companies that have been recommended to me by other authors are Create Space and Ingram Spark. If this is the way you wish to go, be sure to do your research.

5. Think Like a Child – Write Like an Adult

One of the advantages of writing for children is that you have permission to think like a child and get away with it. How do children think? If you have to ask that question, you might want to spend a little more time with children before attempting to write for them. For me, one of the privileges of being a teacher, a mother, and now a grandmother, has been experiencing firsthand the magical world called "childhood."

With respect to the world of children's picture books, we are usually focusing on toddlerhood through second grade. This is a pretty wide span; however, to varying degrees, my findings will fit all these stages. Here are some of my observations about how children think:

Children are enthusiastic. They are eager to know what is coming next in a story. They are excited when good things happen to the characters, their imaginations allowing them almost to live in the world of the story.

Children are creative. Ask them what they think will come next in a story, and enjoy their answers! When I read my unpublished manuscripts to children, I often make changes based on what the children have suggested or envisioned.

Children are self-centered. They enjoy reading stories that relate to them. They like when they can picture themselves as the character in a story they are reading. To see this in action, read a story about super heroes to a kindergarten class, and then watch how many of them go "flying" around the room.

Children love illustrations. Children thrive on visual stimulation. They love bright, colorful illustrations. They prefer pages with more picture than words. Try this: Tell children about a giraffe driving a car, and then show them a cute picture of what you have just described. You will see a huge difference in the reactions.

Children need relatable descriptions. It's not enough simply to say, "the sweater was soft" or "the noise was loud." Children have a clearer understanding of descriptions like "soft as a puppy" or "loud as a whistle."

Children have strong emotions. If you've spent time with children, you know they can be giggling one minute and throwing a screaming tantrum the next minute. A good story will tap into their positive emotions and create pleasant feelings. Give young readers a book filled with silliness and humor, or a satisfying feel-good ending, and they will beg to have it read over and over.

Children love adjectives. Of course they don't know what an adjective is; however, they will react far more positively to a description of a "roly-poly yellow duck" than to just a "yellow duck." Be creative with your adjectives; don't be boring. You can add to the children's vocabularies by adding a few words that are a little less common yet still easy for them to pronounce and understand. Instead of "a big monster," how about a "hurly-burly monster"? Be careful about using double adjectives, such as "a smiling, happy boy." Both words say the same thing, and one of your goals with a picture book is to tell your story in as few choice words as possible.

Children live in the present. It's fine to have your story take place over a few days, but when you talk about "three years later" or "when he grew to be a man," children have no point of reference. They are not able to identify with what is happening if your story extends over a long period of time.

Children love happy endings. They are optimistic. I can't think of any reason ever to have a children's book with a sad ending. Let childhood be a time of optimism and fun. I'm not saying you should completely stay away from important issues that children encounter, such as divorce, but stories should offer young readers a resolution and conclude with a sense of hope for the situation.

Children love fantasy. They have no trouble at all believing that chickens can talk or rabbits wear clothes. They have fun believing in make-believe. Let's let them believe as long as possible. How would Dr. Seuss have achieved such greatness if he didn't believe?

Children have short attention spans. For this reason, it's essential to have things happening on each page. This is one of the beauties of a picture book. Both the words and pictures are "talking" and "moving," which gives the young reader a lot to look at.

Children love bathroom humor. Don't be shy about topics such as underwear, poops and farts. They love it all! This is why *The Fart Fairy* is my bestselling book. Oh, and try not to roll your eyes when parents tell you *their* children don't use words like that.

Children love rhyming words. Children love the rhythm of rhyming lines and are often able to memorize a rhyming story after hearing it just a few times. They also love repetition and alliteration (when the beginning sounds of words are repeated). This is yet another reason why Dr. Seuss books will always be popular.

Example of repetition: Fly, fly, fly in the sky, sky, sky.
Example of alliteration: The green grass grew as the golden goose grinned.

If you would like to write for youngsters, find a group of kids, sit on the floor, talk to them and—above all—listen!

6. Every Story Starts with an Idea: Is Yours a Good One?

While talking to the book-loving people I meet wherever I go, I have been asked many times where my story ideas come from. I'm also asked the question, "Why didn't *I* think of that?" I tell them that stories are everywhere! Just open your eyes—and your imagination—and try to think like a child. Before you know it, someone will say to *you*, "Why didn't *I* think of that?"

Where Do Ideas Come From?

Ideas come from simple, everyday situations that we all deal with, like tangled hair and missing socks. Here are some questions to ponder that just might lead you to discover that great idea you are searching for:

What are some of your favorite childhood experiences? Roller-skating to the grocery store? Sleepovers at Grandma's house? Catching fireflies in a jar? Just be sure your ideas from the past are still relevant today.

What made you happy as a child? Canoeing? Eating ice cream? Going to the movies? Seeing a mountain? Riding on a tractor?

What made you unsure? What made it better? Were you afraid when you went to sleep-away camp? Did you feel better when Mom or Dad came on visiting day? How about going to the hospital? Was everyone friendly, and did they make you feel better? How did you feel on your first day of school?

What did you dream of being when you grew up? A doctor? A farmer? An athlete? An astronaut? A rocket scientist? A marine biologist? Unusual occupations can be woven into interesting stories for first and second graders.

If an animal could do a silly or magical thing, what would it be? Could a pony turn into a unicorn at night? Could a lizard eat your clarinet? Could a cow jump over the moon?

Why do you love snow? Or Summer? Or the beach? Or Grandpa? Or kittens? Or bulldozers? Or frogs?

If you were going to create a super hero, what power would he/she have? Be super fast? Be super strong? Able to leap over a house? Able to fly without wings? Able to see in the dark?

Which Comes First, the Idea or the Audience?

Before you delve any further into the writing process, you will first need to determine both your idea and your audience. For example, if you already have your idea and your goal is to write a story about pandas, you can then decide on your audience and write it specifically for them. A panda story for three-year-olds will be much different than one geared to first graders. Or, if you choose your audience first, such as second grade, you can talk to second graders: See what they are reading and where their interests lie; let their answers help lead you to an idea. You need to know *who* you are writing for *before* you write a book so the story can be carefully tailored to the specific age range.

Once you have your story idea, examine it carefully. Will children like it? As the book publishing world becomes increasingly competitive, it is more important than ever for authors and publishers to understand and properly address their target markets. In most cases the person purchasing a book is the one who will be reading it, but that is not so in the case of picture books. Will your idea appeal to both the person who is buying it and the one who will be reading it?

When you feel comfortable with your idea and have thought of the story you would like to tell, it's time to put this idea into words. This is just a first draft, so don't strive for perfection yet—there's plenty of time for that. Once you have committed it to paper (or, more likely, your computer), the journey has begun. Now is the time to ask yourself these questions:

Is my idea easily understandable? While I was working on my first children's book, *The Knot Fairy*, I organized several decidedly unorganized focus groups consisting of all the children in my daughter's neighborhood. I can now tell you from experience that children are honest, maybe brutally so. What did I learn? I learned that the ending to my book (an ending that I thought made perfect sense) didn't make sense to the ones who would be reading (or hearing) it. Luckily, these little Einsteins had wonderful ideas for what the ending should have been. I can now say with pride that the last line in *The Knot Fairy* was actually written by a seven-year-old! (I'm also proud to say that seven-year-old was my granddaughter, Lindsay.) A few revisions later, I read the book to the same group, this time receiving an enthusiastic "thumbs up." Five book awards later, I think they were right on target. Be humble; don't be afraid to ask. And, if it's "broke"—fix it!

Who is my target audience? If you are writing for toddlers and preschoolers, the vocabulary and illustrative details will not be the same as if you are writing for first and second graders. Even though picture books are enjoyed by both of these age groups, there is a vast difference in comprehension and attention span between toddlers and second graders. Once you have narrowed down your audience, read all the books you can find that were written for that particular age group. Take note of the vocabulary and approximate number of words on each page.

Will my idea appeal to my target audience? It's wise to share your ideas and first draft with the people you are hoping will be the ones to choose your book from a crowded bookstore shelf. I have spoken to several children's authors who said they didn't share their ideas beforehand because they were actually afraid of the results; the thought of receiving negative comments was more than they could bear. All the more reason to do it! One author told me she didn't show her book to anyone because she wanted the story to be a surprise. She "just knew" everyone would love it. Some authors find out too late that it isn't enough to simply feel sure that your audience will love your book. Share it with your target audience and see!

Is my idea timeless? Will readers still "get it" five or ten years from now? There are some aspects of a book that will naturally be out of date in the future, such as the characters' clothes and some of their belongings, and we can't help that. However, there are reasons why the classic books are here to stay. The ideas themselves are timeless. Take a trip to the library and reread (just to name a few) *The Little Prince, Where The Wild Things Are, The Pokey Little Puppy, Are You My Mother?, The Giving Tree,* or any of the Dr. Seuss books, and you will see what I mean.

Is my idea age-appropriate? You probably wouldn't want to write a book with talking baby bunnies as the main characters if you are targeting fifth or sixth graders. On the flip side, you wouldn't expect kindergarten children to understand the books about relationships that middle school readers crave.

As logical as this sounds, I have seen books displaying both incorrect scenarios.

Will children relate to my characters? Here's another example of a near miss: While working on my second book, I thought I now knew everything about how to please children. I thank my lucky stars I came to my senses and called my little focus group together. My story was a perky, rhyming account of *The Button Fairy,* the one responsible for missing buttons. The children hated it! Why? Not one of the children in my group had ever lost a button. They didn't know what I was talking about. In fact, there were twelve children in the group and not one of them even had a single button on their clothes. Zippers, yes. Velcro, yes. Snaps, yes. Buttons, no! My research had shown that, sadly (for me), the book will spend its life on my hard drive and will probably never see the light of day. I went on to another idea. Thank you, kids.

Is it a "feel good" story? Young children love to read and be read to. Stories make them feel good. Tell your idea or read your manuscript to a group of children and watch their faces. Have you given them something to smile about? Are the characters in your story involved in happy events? Do they accomplish pleasant things that other children feel they, too, can accomplish? Are the conversations in your story ones that any child can relate to and feel good about?

The message here is simple: Don't skimp on research; it's free! Find out what the audience you are trying to capture is actually reading. Create a focus group of nieces, nephews, neighbors, etc. Ask kindergarten teachers if they will allow you to visit their classrooms to read your story. I have done this on numerous occasions and have been welcomed each time. In most cases, the teachers have, of course, wanted to read the story first, offering yet another opportunity to gain one more valid opinion.

Talk to bookstore employees. Be sure also to ask them what is NOT selling. Talk to librarians. What are the most popular children's picture books? Check Amazon. What are the best-sellers? What do parents want to read to young children? Find out what the best-selling books all have in common. Then make yours better.

Books referenced in this section:

The Little Prince
by Antoine de Saint-Exupéry

Where The Wild Things Are
by Maurice Sendak

The Pokey Little Puppy
by Janette Sebring Lowrey

Are You My Mother?
by P.D. Eastman

The Giving Tree
by Shel Silverstein

7. Let's Write it Right!
Part One:
What Type of Picture Book Will You Write?

Picture books can play a number of different roles: They may teach a lesson, explain a concept, tell a story, educate or simply entertain. Within the realm of picture books, you will find several different types, each of which can be adapted to play any one of these roles. The target age levels can also vary within each category, depending on the level of readiness of the readers. It's a good idea to visit the library and take a long, hard look at each type of picture book; then choose the area that appeals to you or works best with your story idea. Perhaps your research will even lead you to a new idea.

Board books. For children ages eighteen months to two years, these books are printed on very heavy stock to meet the demands of active little ones who like to tear pages and chew on corners. These books typically contain twelve to sixteen pages, as opposed to the thirty-two pages in most other picture books. The pictures are the most important element, and there may be from zero words to just a few words on each page. There is really no story or plot, just brightly colored illustrations that are simple and one-dimensional. Topics may include shapes, animals (usually more common types, such as puppies, kittens or bunnies), or children doing simple tasks, like brushing their teeth or putting on a hat and mittens.

Concept books. For children ages two to five, these books introduce children to a specific theme, such as the alphabet, counting, colors or shapes. The illustrations are a little more intricate than those in board books, with usually just one illustrated object to match each word or letter of the alphabet.

Wordless books. For children ages three to seven, these books tell the story completely with pictures. Children get to create the stories to go with the illustrations, making the reading of these books a good pre-literacy activity that encourages the use of imagination. The goal of these books is to motivate beginning readers and teach them to look for the clues presented by the illustrations.

Picture books. For children ages four to seven, these are books in which the pictures are as important as the words. The illustrations are, in fact, vital to the books in that they tell half the story. These books can be either fiction or non-fiction. There is one main plot to the story, and there are no subplots; however, the information offered by the illustrations is often enough to be considered a subplot of its own. Picture books that rhyme are among the favorites of children in this age group, who love rhyming, repetition and alliteration.

Picture story books. For children ages seven to nine, these books bridge the gap between picture books and the next big step—chapter books. Similar in style to picture books, there are more words and fewer illustrations; however, the text and pictures still work together to tell the story. In addition, the plots and characters are more complex than those in the picture books described above, and subplots are often used. At this age, children are interested in both fiction and non-fiction books, yet still love fantasy and humor, with "bathroom humor" being among their favorites.

Be sure your book is written for the age group you are targeting.

7. Let's Write it Right!
Part Two:
Get Ready to Write

If you want to be a writer, you have to read and write. This doesn't mean what you think. Of course you can read and write. But two of the best ways to learn how to write picture books are by reading them and by writing them. The reading can be done at your local library. Read as many picture books as you can. As for the writing, if you have been writing all your life and have a drawer or computer crammed with stories, you may be ready to go. For everyone else, I highly suggest that you start by writing a few practice stories. This is a perfect time to find a focus group of children and join (or form) a local writing group. Read your stories to others, and listen carefully to what they have to say.

Find the time to write. If you are ready to take the plunge, plan your writing schedule. Unlike a job with set hours, working on your own really takes discipline. Can you set aside a few hours each morning? Is evening your preferred time? When I first started working from home, I found that all too often entire days would go by without me being able to write even one word. I had the ideas, but at home the doorbell would buzz, the phone would ring, the laundry would be calling to me, or I just had to catch up on the TV show I had recorded the night before. I finally had a talk with myself, and together we (or I) figured it out. Mornings became my scheduled writing time. You can be flexible, but try to stick with a plan—at least in the beginning—and it will soon become routine. If you have small children, finding time to write can be even more difficult; their nap time may be the only quiet time you have to yourself.

Find your own space. If you can, find a dedicated space in your home that you can call your own. Maybe it's just a corner, but let it be *your* corner. Any place where you can keep all your papers spread out in just the right "messy order" is ideal. Some days it's tough enough to get started without having to unpack a laptop, notes, illustrations and other tools of the trade that you packed up the day before when your family reclaimed the kitchen table.

When was the last time you actually read a children's picture book? Could it be time for a trip to the library?

7. Let's Write it Right!
Part Three:
Some Nitty-Gritty, Oh-So-Important Details

As you get ready to write, there are some very important details about picture books to keep in mind. The format and rules are different than with other types of books.

Every good story needs a beginning, a middle and an end. Every story, including those in picture books, needs these three elements. In the beginning of the story, we are introduced to the main characters or situation; in the middle, the action reaches a climax; at the end, the situation is resolved. If one of these three major elements is missing, your story is not complete.

Write a strong opening. The first sentence is extremely important. Because a picture book has relatively few words overall, it's especially important to make the opening ones count. The first sentence needs to be so inviting that it will capture the attention of the readers and make them want to learn more. An example of a boring opening is, "The sun was shining as I walked to school." So what? An example of a more interesting opening might be, "A lizard lives in my desk at school." That would likely attract a lot more interest. An intriguing question can also make a good opening sentence: "Have you ever held a caterpillar in your hand?" My book, *The Freckle Fairy*, begins with the question, "Do you think it's true that fairies have freckles just like you and me?" A good question will make children want to read the book to find the answer. Try writing a few different openers, and run them by your focus group.

Picture books almost always have thirty-two pages. This is the industry standard. The reason for the page count is a result of the traditional method of paper cutting that printers have used for many years and is still in use today. When the printer folds large sheets of paper, each folds neatly into eight pages, resulting in a page count of multiples of eight. Occasionally you will come across a picture book that is more or less than thirty-two pages, however it will still be in multiples of eight. Included in the count are the title page, copyright page and dedication page. In all, you will have sixteen two-sided pages to fill. (Note: This is not true of e-books, which can be of any length since folded paper is not an issue.)

The plots are simple. As adults, we know what it is like to read a great novel or mystery and follow the characters through several decades and many plot changes. Young children are not ready to deal with subplots or stories that take multiple twists and turns. Choose your main plot and stay with it to the end. If your story teaches a lesson, stick with that one lesson.

The ending brings resolution. Whatever story you tell or lesson you teach, it needs to have a satisfying resolution. Children shouldn't be left wondering whatever happened to the puppy who was trying to find his way home, or the little girl who was worried about getting on the big yellow bus. Wrap it up neatly and in a way that will make the young readers feel good.

The characters are simple. The challenge is to create a main character that is simple, yet compelling. You want young readers to identify with the character and feel the same emotions that the character is feeling. Create someone (it can be a human or an animal) with a personality and a point of view, and not simply a flat drawing on a page. Children love to read about characters who have an "attitude." The other characters in the story are also important, and their personalities are often depicted by who they are: pesky little sister or brother, frolicking family pet, etc. You need to know the personality traits of your characters even though you will generally not be describing them with words. Much of it will be done with the illustrations, so communicate the character traits well to your illustrator. A good illustrator will be able to portray your characters in a way that makes a clear statement about who they are and what they are feeling.

Delete all unnecessary words. One way to do this is to keep your descriptions short; another way is to avoid using double adjectives. Make sure each and every word is necessary to the understanding of the story. Remember, young children have short attention spans. Most are learning to read by figuring out one letter at a time, so you don't want to overwhelm them. One or two lines of text per page is perfect for toddlers and beginning readers. In most cases, picture books will have about 500 words per book, or sixteen words per page. If you are targeting slightly older children, such as first and second graders, up to four lines of text (up to 1000 words per book) will work. At this age, they are able to grasp slightly more complex story plots, but be sure your story is captivating enough to hold their interest. Don't run the risk of being boring. I have kept my books to 300 words or less. My theory is: Get in, tell an enchanting story and get out!

Don't use slang. It's important to refrain from using slang or regional words in your story. Your goal should be to have your book appeal to *all* children. It would be a mistake to use words that people in other parts of the county (and other parts of the world) may not understand or may even interpret as racial or cultural stereotyping.

Be careful with dialogue. As adults, we have all read novels with so much dialogue that we have to stop, go back, and reread entire sections to figure out who said what. This confusion happens more readily to beginning readers, who can easily become lost if there is too much back and forth dialogue. This doesn't mean you have to omit it altogether. Using dialogue is fine as long as you make it simple, short and clear.

Choose an easy-to-read font. Choose carefully. This is not an area where you want to try to be cute. Avoid hard-to-read fonts with curlicue letters that may confuse young children. Children learn to read with basic letter forms and may not recognize some of the variations in letters.

> *Example*:
>
> g vs. **g**
>
> The second one is a better choice for beginning readers.

Choice of fonts. The easiest-to-read and most commonly used fonts for children's picture books are ones like **Helvetica** or **Futura**. These are known as *sans serif* and are less fancy, more rounded and easier to read than the *serif* fonts, such as **Times New Roman** and **Georgia**. Definitely avoid using words with all capital letters, as well as hyphenated words, again to avoid confusion.

Font color. The norm for text color in books, whether for children or adults, is black. Children are usually taught to read books that have black text on a white background; other colors have been found to be distracting, even with older readers. You can add lots of color with your illustrations; don't try to be fancy with different text colors.

Font size. The size of the font in most children's picture books is 14-point, large enough for most children to see clearly. Larger fonts may be used in some books for toddlers, especially the very early books with only one or two words to a page.

Is now the time to write in rhyme? Rhyming books are especially difficult to write. Children love them, but not every writer is able to create a good rhyme. The words must really rhyme. Please don't try to force words to rhyme. If words don't rhyme, they don't rhyme. For example, "rose" and "toads" do not rhyme! A good rhyming dictionary may help you come up with some better words. Be careful, though: Don't use words that do rhyme but whose meanings don't fit the story!

Then, there's the rhythm. The rhythm pattern should be consistent throughout the book. A rhyme without rhythm just doesn't work. I have seen many books where the words rhyme, but the rhythm of the lines is weak. In this case, sometimes adding or deleting extra syllables can make a huge difference.

Example:
So all of the fairies helped her pack up her supplies,
And she had goggles on her eyes.
vs.
So the fairies all help her to pack her supplies,
Including the goggles she wears on her eyes.

You should be able to feel how much better the rhythm is in the second rhyme.

If you are having difficulty with your own rhyming and rhythm, remember that a story written in good prose is much better than one written in poor rhyme. Poor rhymes are like fingernails on a chalkboard!

So now that we've addressed the fundamentals, head down to the children's section of your nearest library. Pull a stack of picture books from the shelves, and check out these ideas in action. A few afternoons of library research will make you an expert at these nitty-gritty, but oh-so-important details.

Once all of this has been done, you can relax a bit and enjoy the journey.

8. It's Time to Make a Mock-Up Book

When you feel comfortable with your story, and your focus groups have given it an initial thumbs up, it's time to make a mock-up of the book. This simply means to cut paper to the projected size of your book (9 x 9 inches, 8.5 x 11 inches, and so forth). Don't staple it together yet; rather, spread the pages on a table. If you are writing a standard thirty-two-page book, be sure you have thirty-two pages that include a title page, dedication page and copyright page. Type your story in size fourteen font and cut out the words, arranging them in order on the blank pages. This is a way to see if the story flows and if each page makes sense on its own.

Read through the mock-up several times; you might find yourself rearranging the order of the words. If yours is a rhyming book, this will help you see how the placement of the words can affect the "timing of the rhyming." Make sure each page begins and ends in a logical place. This is extremely important. Your goal for each page is to leave the reader wondering what comes next. This is also the time to add or delete words as needed and double-check for clarity.

Now you can staple it together and even add your own sketch ideas on each page. These notes and sketches will come in handy when you meet with your illustrator. Read the book again to your friends or focus group. Again, listen to what they have to say.

Sample Mock-Up Book

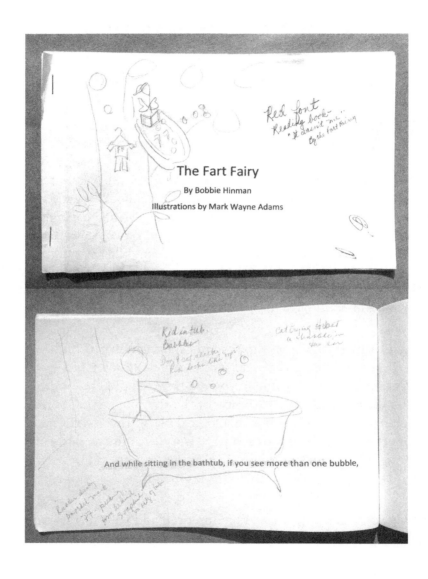

9. And the Title is...

O ne of the most important tasks in creating a book is coming up with the perfect title. Your content may be great, but without a good title, potential readers may not pay attention to your book. Many authors choose a title for their book before they even start writing. Others may come up with their title later in the process. Either way, try thinking of it as a "working title," meaning exactly what it says: The book is a work in progress, and so is the title. As you write the book, and often after you finish writing, your ideas for a title will likely change a few times. You may want to keep a log in which you jot down each title as it comes to mind, all to be reviewed at a later date. There's a lot at stake here. The title goes hand-in-hand with the cover in forming your prospective readers' first impressions of the book.

If you are struggling with the choice of a title, here are a few suggestions to guide you:

Brainstorm with friends. Talking with others about your theme and the characters in the book may help you form an idea. Jot down the key words that come to mind as you toss ideas back and forth, until they start to crystallize.

Meet with your focus group. This is a great project for your focus group, and one they relish. When I visit with my group or an elementary school class, I often play the "Title Game" with them. I read them a list of three or four possible titles. Without telling them what the book is about, I ask them which of the titles they would choose if they were going to choose a book at random. I might start by giving them choices, such as:

A Lizard Came to My House
Lizards Are Funny
My Pet Lizard
A Lizard Ate My Basketball

One of these is actually a working title of mine for a new book. Which one did you choose? If it was the last one, I'm in good shape. That's the one my focus group also chose. I've learned to value their opinions. I have found children's imaginations to be crystal clear, and I listen to what they have to say.

You don't always have to be fancy. Sometimes simply using the name of your character is all you need. Some of the most popular children's books are named this way, such as *Amelia Bedelia* and *Stuart Little*. The first name of a character with one choice adjective also works. Think of *Fancy Nancy* and *Curious George*.

It's okay to be silly. Children love silliness. Some of my favorite popular books have silly titles, such as *Giraffes Can't Dance*, *Sheep in a Jeep* and *Don't Let The Pigeon Drive The Bus*.

Pique their interest. An interesting title can certainly do this. Of course, you have to start with an interesting story. In my example above, have I piqued your interest in my book titled *A Lizard Ate My Basketball?*

Longer isn't necessarily better. There have been a number of popular children's books with very long titles. The one that comes to my mind right away is *Alexander and the Terrible, Horrible, No Good, Very Bad Day*. And this works. In fact, I think it's a genius idea for a title. But unless you can come up with a long title that is this captivating, it is better to grab their attention with a short, catchy one.

Be sure you can deliver the ideas your title conveys. If you call your book *The Funny World of Mr. Bunny* and children find nothing funny in the story, you obviously have made a big mistake. If the reader is left trying to figure out the meaning of the title, you've made the wrong choice.

Titles are not exclusive: You can't copyright the title of a book. This is why you sometimes see multiple books with the same title. That said, even if you love the title of another book, it's better to come up with your own. You want your book to stand out and be one-of-a-kind.

It's worth repeating: The title goes hand-in-hand with the cover in forming your prospective readers' first impression of the book.

$a+b=c$

Books referenced in this section:
Amelia Bedelia by Peggy Parish
Stuart Little by E. B. White
Fancy Nancy by Jane O'Connor
Curious George by H. A. Rey
Alexander and the Terrible, Horrible, No Good, Very Bad Day by Judith Viorst
Giraffes Can't Dance by Giles Andreae
Sheep in a Jeep by Nancy E. Shaw
Don't Let The Pigeon Drive The Bus by Mo Willems

$2+2=4$

10. The Very Big Question!

Stop! Before you go any further, ask yourself this question:

What Makes My Book Unique?

What is YOUR Answer to this Question?

This is a question that interviewers, bookstore owners and prospective distributors will likely ask you in the future. At this point, what are your plans to make your book stand out in a crowd of children's picture books? Before you go any further into the process, it may be time to learn the 3Rs:

Review – Reread – Revisit

Review your idea. Does it need a tweak?

Reread your story. Does it need some work?

Revisit your focus group. What are their suggestions?

NOW is the time to make changes in the story, *before* you start the illustration process.

How do You Think You will Answer the VERY BIG QUESTION When Your Book is Complete?

What do you think would be a good answer? *My* answers to this pointed question have resulted in my books being placed in major bookstores around the country. I will share with you the answers I often give:

My book offers—

1) An Audio CD featuring the story narration and an original song

2) Rhyming text that is ideal for beginning readers

3) Colorful, attractive covers that are inviting to children

4) Original watercolor illustrations on each page

5) Inclusive characters, featuring boys *and* girls *and* multicultural children

6) Heavy stock to make the books durable and child-friendly

These were *my* answers, but they are not the *only* answers. Your book may have other wonderful and unique features that I wish I had thought of. Keep the BIG question in mind as you go forward because I will ask you this question again later in the book.

Part 2.
The Middle:
A Work in Progress

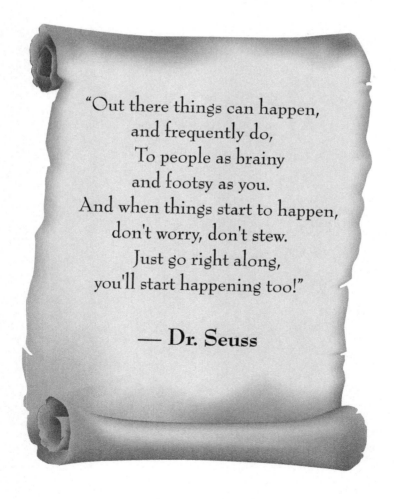

"Out there things can happen,
and frequently do,
To people as brainy
and footsy as you.
And when things start to happen,
don't worry, don't stew.
Just go right along,
you'll start happening too!"

— Dr. Seuss

11. You Will Need to Apply for These...

Once you have finalized your manuscript and are searching for your editor and illustrator, you will need to tend to some very left-brained tasks that are not nearly as much fun as writing. It is now time to apply for the following necessary identifiers for your book:

Copyright: This is the exclusive legal right to reproduce, publish, sell or distribute your book. The current cost is thirty-five dollars, and you can apply online through the Library of Congress website. If you've ever wondered why there may be several books with the same title, it's because book titles themselves cannot be copyrighted. What you are copyrighting is the actual story. Of utmost importance: Be certain when filling out the registration forms that you list *your* name as the claimant of the copyright. If *anyone* else is completing the copyright registration for you, be sure to review the form before it is submitted. Changing information after the copyright is filed can become an expensive nightmare. The notice of copyright should be placed on the copyright page of your book.

In some cases you can *trademark* a title. Very few people do this because unless the U.S. Patent and Trademark Office considers your title a distinctive mark, you will not be granted a trademark. Book titles that become a brand, such as *Harry Potter*, are trademarked.

ISBN (International Standard Book Number): This number uniquely identifies your book and facilitates the sale of your book to bookstores and libraries. Think of it as a Social Security number for your book. Wholesalers and distributors require that books have ISBNs. All libraries and bookstores do, too. The official U.S. agency that supplies ISBNs is Bowker® Identifier Services. You can purchase either one ISBN individually or multiple ISBNs as a block. Currently, the cost of one ISBN is $125, and a block of ten costs $295, so if you are planning to write more than one book, you may want to consider buying the larger quantity. The ISBNs you purchase will not go out of date and can be used at any time. You will need a separate ISBN for each book you publish and, once assigned, the ISBN never changes, even if you make editorial, illustrative or price changes to your book. Once used, an ISBN can never be used again, by you or anyone else. The ISBN should be placed on the back cover of your book and on the copyright page. Read more about the ISBN in the section titled "Who Will Print Your Book?"

LCCN (Library of Congress Control Number): This represents the serial numeric system for cataloging records in the Library of Congress. It's the number that shows that your book exists, and it's the number that any library you are pitching your book to wants to know you have. This number is free and can be obtained online fairly quickly. You must have your ISBN first in order to register for the LCCN. This number should be listed on your copyright page.

CIP (Cataloging in Publication): This is a bibliographic record for your book that looks like a strange combination of letters or numbers (see example). Librarians require very specific information about new titles to facilitate the processing of new books; this includes the determination of the exact shelf location for the materials within the library. The purpose of Cataloging in Publication is to provide librarians with all the information they need in an agreed-upon format and vocabulary. Large publishers have their CIPs prepared by the Library of Congress; however, the premier supplier for small press (ten or fewer books) titles is Quality Books, Inc. They create a CIP almost identical to the ones prepared by the Library of Congress, and their turnaround time is much faster. All Quality Books, Inc. CIP records are entered in the largest cataloging database in the world, the source most U.S. libraries access for their cataloging. This information, although it may look strange, should be copied exactly as it is sent to you and placed on the copyright page of your book. Here is an example of a CIP from one of my books:

Publisher's Cataloging-in-Publication
(Provided by Quality Books, Inc.)

Hinman, Bobbie, author.
    The freckle fairy : book and audio CD / by Bobbie
Hinman ; illustrated by Mark Wayne Adams.
    pages cm + 1 audio disc (digital ; 4 3/4 in.)
    Includes compact disc.
    SUMMARY: In this rhyming book, a mischievous little
fairy flies through the night sky, visiting children as
they sleep, depositing kisses on foreheads, noses and
chins. When the children awaken, they are delighted to
see that a freckle has appeared on each place she has
kissed.
    Audience: Ages 3-7.
    ISBN 978-0-9786791-2-5

    1. Fairies--Juvenile fiction. 2. Freckles--Juvenile
fiction. 3. Stories in rhyme. [1. Fairies--Fiction.
2. Freckles--Fiction. 3. Stories in rhyme.]   I. Adams,
Mark Wayne, 1971- illustrator. II. Title.

PZ8.3.H5564Fre 2016   [E]
                    QBI16-600064

Barcode: Your book will need a barcode. The reason for this is that major retailers, as well as wholesalers and distributors, use a scannable version of the ISBNs in their systems. Barcodes for books are designed to contain both the ISBN of the book and the price. The ISBN is always printed above the barcode symbol. You can order your barcode from Bowker® along with your ISBN, or you can order it when your book is ready to print. Currently, the cost of one barcode is $25. Alternatively, your printer can take care of obtaining the barcode for you and giving it the proper placement on the lower righthand corner of the back cover.

Once all of this has been done, you can relax a bit and enjoy the journey.

12. Make the Cover POP!

How important is the cover of a children's picture book? The answer is: So important that I can't even think of the right word to describe how important it is! I'll try with a few choice adverbs: It is utterly, decidedly, undeniably, unequivocally, absolutely, far and away, beyond any doubt, sure as heck important! The picture book cover *must* reach out and grab you. It must POP! If it could talk, it would have to say, "CHOOSE ME!"

I can say with a great deal of certainty that my fairy book covers have helped me sell so many books. At book festivals and in bookstores, when faced with a multitude of books to choose from, prospective customers will reach for the ones with outstanding covers and catchy titles.

Can You Judge a Book by Its Cover?

We've all heard the well-known expression, "You can't judge a book by its cover." I happen to think a majority of us *do* initially choose a book on the basis of the cover. Like many other shoppers, I reach for the books on the shelf whose covers, I feel, are sending me vibes. The quality and characteristics of the cover may be the deciding factors as to whether or not a prospective customer will choose to take a more in-depth look at a book. If people are in a hurry, perhaps grabbing a book at an airport, the cover may even be the *only* factor they have time to consider. Regrettably, one of the major faults in self-publishing is that too many books have an unprofessional-looking cover.

A poor cover can absolutely ruin the chances of selling a book. I have a sad feeling there are many beautifully written and illustrated books that go unread simply because the cover looks amateurish or uninteresting.

Go to a busy bookstore or library, and watch your target audience. See what *they* choose. When books are displayed with the front cover in full view, what do young children reach for first? Let's take a look at some of the elements involved when a young customer selects a children's picture book:

Color: Children will reach for the bright colors that make covers POP. I have read a number of articles relating to this topic, and most of the writers hold the opinion that children (as well as many adults) are more likely to choose bright, cheerful colors, with red and yellow being among the top choices. Bright colors are "happy" colors.

Subject matter: Children will choose a cover if it "tells them" that what's inside the book is something they like. The cover should offer a little tease of what's inside. If it's a book about trucks, it's not enough just to have the word "truck" in the title. Show the happiest, silliest truck on the cover so the young truck-lover will reach for that book. Stay away from random, generic illustrations. Be sure the character or actions pictured on the cover appear someplace in the book—I guarantee the children will be looking for them.

Pictures: Children love pictures, so be sure the picture on the cover is irresistible. It should be large and colorful and indicate how beautiful the inside art will be. Children *really* love covers that are funny, so having your character doing something comical on the cover is another step in the right direction. Once the cover art has been designed, your cover will be valuable in your marketing campaign. This is one more reason to make it appealing.

Font: Young readers are proud of their reading ability, so make it easy for them. How annoyed are you when you can't make out the words in a title due to an excessively frilly font? Imagine a beginning reader trying to decipher a title printed in 𝕺𝖑𝖉 𝕰𝖓𝖌𝖑𝖎𝖘𝖍, for example. The title font can be a little decorative and playful, but it must be easy to read. There's also what I call "the 6-foot rule": You should be able to read the title of a children's picture book from 6 feet away. I don't know who said it, and I doubt if it's been scientifically proven, but I believe it to be true.

Placement: Children read from left to right (in the English language). Adults do, too; however, our adult eyes and brains are able to process a larger area at one time. My first illustrator taught me that, for this reason, it's best to have the illustration on the left side of the cover and the title on the right; you want the children's eyes to go directly to the bright, comical character on the left and fall instantly in love.

Who Will Design the Cover?

Another choice you will have to make is deciding who will actually design your cover. There are book design companies that specialize in this area and will work with you in creating your cover. You can also find companies selling "stock" covers that can sometimes be customized to fit your needs. If you go either of these routes, be sure the cover includes actual artwork from your book, rather than generic characters that have nothing to do with your story.

I prefer to have my illustrator design the art for the cover, with the graphic designer then arranging the illustration and text in an appealing way. This will make the cover art consistent with the inside illustrations, adding continuity to the book. With my first book I was able to form a working relationship with my illustrator and designer and have gone this route with all of my subsequent book covers. Each time, the cover was the first element the illustrator created. Her illustration was then sent to the designer, who "did his magic." The designer was also able to show me examples of several different fonts, along with a few different cover layouts from which to choose.

In many cases, your budget will ultimately be one of the important factors in deciding who will create your cover. Do your homework and carefully compare the costs and services different designers will provide. Keep the important elements in mind and choose carefully. This is not a place to sacrifice quality.

Now, add this to your homework: Go into a bookstore and look at the covers of lots of picture books. Which ones jump out at you? Which are the prettiest, funniest or most intriguing? Once you've decided what it is about them that you like the most, make a plan for what elements you'd like used in *your* book cover.

What About the Back Cover?

Don't forget the back cover. Make sure you include this in the contract with your cover designer. If your book's front cover has done its job of reaching out and grabbing your buyers, the back cover is the next thing they look at when deciding whether or not to make a purchase. There are a few important features to include on the back cover of a picture book:

Design features from the front cover. Important design features, like the colors, borders, background and images, should continue on the back. The "feel" of the book should remain the same.

An image. Include an illustration of the main character, smaller than the one on the front cover, and perhaps in a different pose. Your illustrator can design a small spot-illustration that would be perfect to use here. (See the section titled "It's All About the Pictures.")

A short promotional description. Include a short—and tempting— description of the book and, if the space allows, a very brief author bio. If the cover initially caught a shopper's attention, this is the place to reel them in and clinch the sale.

Quotes praising your book or series. If this is your first book, you probably do not have reviews yet; however, a quote from a well-known person is nice when possible. A quote from an unknown person, such as a relative or your first grade teacher, would be meaningless and a wrong choice; it's better not to have any quotes. If this is your second book, you can use quotes from the first book, but only if they are meaningful. After you become famous, you will have lots of testimonials.

Cover art from a previous book, if applicable. If you have written previous books, a nice addition would be to include pictures of their covers; if these books have received awards, this information can also be listed.

Logo. An attractive logo adds a professional touch to a back cover. There are online companies that offer easy design tools. Alternatively, most illustrators and graphic designers will be able to work with you in creating a logo. You may even be creative enough to design it yourself.

Barcode. In most cases, the barcode is added by the printer. Just be sure the cover designer leaves a space for it in the lower righthand corner.

Price. The barcode will contain the price; however, some authors add the price in a more readable form just above the barcode. This is not necessary, and can actually be a problem if you later change the price of the book. A barcode sticker with the new price can easily cover the existing barcode, but the old price will still visible above.

And Don't Forget the Spine

The spine is the skinny, vertical back edge of the book. Like the back cover, it should reflect the colors of the front cover. It should contain the title, your last name and your logo. A subtitle is not printed on the spine. It's a small space, so the text should be as large as will properly fit and still be legible. Make sure that when the book is lying flat with the front cover facing up, the lettering on the spine is right-side up; having titles all facing the same direction makes it easier to read when they are lined up on a bookstore or library shelf.

And the Dust Jacket

If your book is going to be published in hardcover format, the addition of a dust jacket would be like the icing on the cake. The dust jacket is printed to look exactly like the cover and with the same finish (either matte or gloss) as the book. What I love about the dust jacket, aside from the richness it adds to a book, are the folded flaps that hold it to the cover. These flaps give the author more space to add information about the book. Here you can add a longer bio and book summary (blurb) to replace or supplement the ones on the back cover. In this case, you can either omit the ones on the back or keep them very short. There is also room on the flaps to add information about the illustrator and designer.

Your book cover design will play a large part in a bookstore buyer taking your book seriously and making the decision to carry it.

13. Do You Really Need an Editor?

Editing is a *very* important step in the creation of a book. Unfortunately, this is an area where many self-publishing authors try to save money. Hiring an editor may seem like a waste of time and money to you, but every writer needs an extra set of eyes.

Can you edit your own book? Sure. *Should* you edit your own book? No! Then who should do the editing? An editor! Not your best friend who loves to read, not your nephew who has always had "straight As" in English, and definitely not YOU! There are multiple reasons why your friends should not edit your work. They may not be qualified, and they may not want to hurt your feelings if they see something they think should be changed. As for your nephew, he is most likely not qualified, and I'll stop there. As for you, the author, no matter how proficient you are in grammar and sentence structure, you cannot be objective. You are also likely to see what you think should be there and gloss over any errors or omissions.

You need an editor's help in three main areas:
1. To look for typos, along with grammar and punctuation errors
2. To make sure you have chosen the best word to fit each idea or concept you are presenting
3. To look at the story as a whole to be sure it makes sense and is easy to understand

Why Does a PICTURE Book Need Editing?

I've often been asked why an editor is needed for a children's picture book when there are so few words in the book. That's just it. Every book needs to be edited, even if there are only ten words on a page. Because there are fewer words, every word counts. The use of one word can alter the meaning of an entire page, so making sure you have the correct meaning is just as important as having the correct spelling.

What Does the Editing Process Involve?

I prefer to start the ball rolling relatively early in the process. I like to run my early manuscript by my editor and get her initial opinions of the idea and characters. When I have finished writing the story, and feel it's complete, the editing process actually begins. The editor corrects any grammar and punctuation errors, and offers suggestions for word replacement that she feels would benefit the story. When this has been completed, my manuscript is ready for the illustrator. Then, when the first illustration sketches are available, I show my editor how it will all fit together and how the story and words intertwine. This is also when I submit to her the text that will go on the front and back covers and the dust jacket. At this point, text changes can still be made. Last, before the book goes to print, while it is still in the hands of the graphic designer, and errors can still be corrected, she proofreads the entire book.

How Do You Find an Editor?

There are numerous websites where editors are listed along with their areas of expertise and their qualifying experiences. There are also sites where you can post a description of what you are looking for, and editors who are interested will send you their resumes. You can easily contact the ones that interest you and ask for references and titles of works they have edited.

Try to follow up by contacting some of their former clients. If you are able to attend a large book fair or an event like BookExpo (formerly known as Book Expo America), you will be able to talk to other authors and self-publishers about their choice of editors, and also be able to look at the work they have produced. Find an editor who specializes in children's books. Editors' fees vary, with some editors charging by the hour and others charging by the word. In my experience, I have found the editing fees for children's picture books to be much lower than the fees for a chapter book. You should be able to find an editor to fit your needs and your budget.

Ask yourself a question: What if you do your own editing and miss an error? Will it haunt you? It's better to do it right at the outset.

BookExpo is the largest publishing event in North America. Formerly known as Book Expo America (or BEA), their yearly convention is attended by authors, booksellers, librarians, educators, publishers and specialty retailers from all over the globe, and features everything current in the literary world.

14. It's All About the Pictures!
Part One: What You Need to Know About the Illustrations

I've said it before and I'll say it again: Do your research! Research is free, so don't skimp. The library and your local bookstore are the best places for this task. Look at lots of picture books. Which illustrations and formats do you like best? Is there a color scheme that you favor? Take notes on everything you like and everything you dislike. There are many factors to be considered when planning the illustrations for a picture book.

In almost every case, the illustrator retains the copyright to the illustrations, along with ownership of the original artwork. The author is normally granted a license to use the artwork in the book for which it was created, along with any marketing for the book. This agreement is normally in effect for the life of the book. Any contract that you enter into must have all the provisions stated clearly. Also, be sure you and the illustrator agree on the date by which the artwork is to be finished, and state it in the contract. (To be on the safe side, it's a good idea for both you and the illustrator to have your lawyers look over any contract before you sign.)

Details to Consider Before You Begin

The illustrations play an important role. This is a picture book. It's all about having the pictures and the words join together to present the story, the role of each being to tell its share. And, it's about finding the perfect balance between the two elements.

The words in a picture book are simple; the illustrations can be more complex. For example, while the text in *The Knot Fairy* tells you the fairy "ties little knots one after another…," the picture shows children with knotted hair, a dog with knotted whiskers, and a cat and mouse each with a knot in their tail. Compare the number of words you would need to describe all this in detail with the ability of one well-done illustration to do the job. Now imagine the joy on the faces of the children as they discover the telltale knots.

The illustrations must match the words. This is crucial, yet I've seen so many books exhibit the contrary. Why would you talk about visiting Grandma for Christmas and have the illustration on that page be a horse in a pasture? Yes, I actually saw this! The illustrations must match the words! There, I've said it twice. Remember, you are striving for the perfect balance between pictures and words. It isn't balanced if a picture has little or nothing to do with the words. As you plan your illustrations, remember how important this is to the understanding and enrichment of the story.

The size of the illustrations should be considered. Your research will help you decide whether you prefer full-page illustrations or predominantly white pages with spot illustrations. I have also seen another version where one page is white and contains just the words, while the facing page has the illustration. The decision is yours. Personally, I prefer full-page illustrations (the bigger, the better). After all, it *is* a picture book.

The action goes from left to right. This should always be the case. We read text from left to right, so it makes sense that we also "read" pictures in the same way. The action and words on the left-hand page should guide the reader to the right-hand page. The action and words on the right-hand page should then lead readers to turn to the next page, piquing their interest in what is coming next.

You can choose individual illustrations or spreads. This is another decision. A spread is when two facing pages are illustrated as one. If both the left-hand and right-hand illustrations share a common background, you may want to consider a spread. Of course, if the main character appears on both pages, a spread would not work; no one can be in two places at once. I like the fluidity of spreads; however, in all of my books I have a combination of both concepts, according to what the storyline dictates.

The word placement must be carefully planned. Should the words be at the top or bottom of the page? I don't know of any hard-and-fast rules that dictate the word placement. Sometimes it depends on the illustrations. Some authors mix it up and use a combination of text placements. I've always felt that it is easier for beginning readers to follow text that is placed consistently. To me it feels more comfortable to read the words at the bottom and look up at the picture, rather than looking down. Make the decision based on your own story, illustrations and research.

There needs to be ample contrast between words and pictures. If you want full-page illustrations in your book, you and your illustrator will have to plan carefully. Since it's difficult to read words on top of a busy background, the illustrator or graphic designer can erase the section of illustration that will contain the words, giving that area what I call a "cotton ball effect." If you are just using spot illustrations, it's still important to leave a good solid space for the text. There should never be words against a dark background or one with busy patterns or objects.

No one wants to fall in the gutter! Gutters in picture books refer to the place where the binding connects two pages. Seasoned illustrators are usually aware of this and are careful when designing the artwork to not have important illustration elements fall into the gutter.

Extra details can add excitement. The pictures can tell the reader things that the words don't say. Look for places to add these extra details. For example, a simple street scene in a book can be made very exciting by adding people and pets looking out of the house windows, children on bikes, roller skates on the sidewalk, a school bus riding by and even a helicopter in the sky. Discoveries such as these are always exciting to children.

The continuity of elements is important. In most cases, it's a good idea to have your main characters appear on each page (or each spread). It's also a good idea to add a few items that can be repeated throughout the book. I like to give my characters props, such as a unique hat, backpack, flashlight, teddy bear, doll, etc. If your main character is an animal, the props might be a bone, a sock monkey, or anything amusing that relates to the character. These become items of interest as they appear in different arrangements throughout the book. An image or background near the front of a book can also be repeated later to create continuity. In *The Fart Fairy*, my character travels with a pet skunk who appears on every page. In *The Belly Button Fairy*, a dog, cat, teddy bear and parrot appear in various silly poses throughout the book. Be creative and think about what interesting items you can place on each page.

There are different media your illustrator might choose. Many children's books are illustrated in watercolor. In addition to the vivid colors, this medium also provides such lovely, soft textures. I've actually watched people open my books and run their hands across the illustrations, expecting to be able to feel the texture. Many illustrators seem to be moving towards digital coloring, which can be very beautiful and appealing as well. Some illustrators work with colored pencils, others with pen and ink. I've even seen books illustrated with beautiful cut-paper designs. It's important to discuss this with your illustrator and use the medium he or she is most comfortable with, thereby producing the best work possible. Every medium can be scanned and converted into a digital file for printing.

You have a choice of your book size and format. You will need to decide the size and shape of your book before you actually plan the illustrations. How do you envision your book? If your story is about tall buildings or dinosaurs, perhaps a vertical book would work best with the illustrations. If there will be lots of characters or houses, or even a train, perhaps a horizontal book would be best. There are also square books. A very popular size, whether horizontal or vertical, is 8.5 x 11 inches.

14. It's All About the Pictures!
Part Two: How to Find the Perfect Illustrator

This, to me, was the crucial step in creating my picture books. Would I find another person who shared my vision? Would there be anyone who could transfer to paper what I was picturing in my head? My search began. What I now know that I didn't know in the beginning was how little I knew! An experienced book illustrator will guide you through the process instead of the other way around.

In traditional publishing, the illustrator is chosen by the publisher, with authors often having little or no choice in the matter. With self-publishing, the choice of illustrators is up to the author. So, where do you start?

Nearby colleges or art schools. There are many talented art students who would love the experience of illustrating a book. The potential problem here is that they will need guidance because they might not be familiar with illustrating for a story as opposed to creating individual pieces of art. If this is your first picture book, you may want to choose a more experienced book illustrator.

Yourself or your family? I have seen many picture books illustrated by the author or a family member. I have to be perfectly honest when I say that, in most cases, the final products, while nice, just do not look professional. Now, to contradict myself: We all need to be aware that the famous Dr. Seuss wrote and illustrated his famous books, as did Maurice Sendak, who wrote *and* illustrated *Where the Wild Things Are*. So, anything can happen!

Book fairs. I mention this a lot because visiting book fairs will put you in touch with other self-published authors. Look at their books. If you see an illustrator's work that strikes your fancy, ask for the person's contact information. Be sure to also ask if the illustrator was easy to work with, finished the project on time, etc.

The Internet. My initial search took me to the Internet. I began by Googling "children's illustrators." I also searched for "fairy illustrators," since my books are all about fairies. When I started the process I had no idea what type of illustrations I wanted; however, I could picture in my mind what I wanted my main character to look like. But did I want realistic drawings or more fanciful ones? Did I like cartoon-like characters? I wasn't sure. I looked at literally hundreds of online portfolios until BINGO, one of the characters living happily in a portfolio was exactly what I had pictured in my mind. I sent emails to this illustrator, and also to several others whose work I found appealing. I had done plenty of research, so by now I knew the specifics of a children's picture book. I was able to communicate to the illustrators what my project would entail: illustrations for a children's picture book with thirty-two pages, full-page artwork for the insides and the cover, art for the endpapers, and a few spot illustrations for the title page, back cover and CD. I also let them know what the story was about and that I would like the finished book to measure 8.5 x 11 inches in horizontal format. (This is a popular size and one that is a personal preference of mine.) I also inquired about the time frame required and—of utmost importance—the price.

I was happy to receive a response from each illustrator. Most had itemized their fees for each full page and each spot illustration, then provided a grand total. In a few cases, the fee was truly grand! Fortunately, the illustrator whose work I loved the most fit my budget. If you don't find the right illustrator in your first search, search again. There are so many talented artists out there, and it's worth the effort to find the right one.

Once you have found the person you feel is right for you, you will need to sign a contract describing each of your responsibilities, along with a list of all costs involved and—again of utmost importance—a deadline date for completion of the illustrations. I would never attempt to offer advice on legal matters, but I do feel it is always wise to have a lawyer look over any contracts you sign.

I can't stress enough how important the illustrations are to your book. After all, it's a *picture* book. Do your research and find the best illustrator you can afford.

14. It's All About the Pictures!
Part Three: Steps in Creating the Illustrations

A lot more goes into creating the illustrations than you have probably imagined. In the best scenario, you and the illustrator will work together, sharing ideas and listening to each other's opinions. The process works best with a give-and-take relationship, as you both have a lot to offer. Always remember that creating a book is a collaborative effort. Every illustrator has his or her own methods and ways of working; however, there are some basic steps to creating the artwork that most will follow.

Before You Begin

Make notes for the illustrator. There are different ways to compile your notes for the illustrator. With my first book, I had already created a cut-and-staple version of the book. (See the section titled "It's Time to Make a Mock-Up Book.") I placed the words on each page, then decided what I thought the best picture would be to go with the words, and scribbled a drawing on each page. I was totally stumped on some of the pages, and that's where the give and take with the illustrator came into play. Together we were able to mesh our ideas. With my later books, I was able to work from the text, visualizing what I thought the characters would be doing. Next to each line of text I wrote my suggestions in red and emailed them to the illustrator. She added her suggestions in blue and sent them back to me. A few times back and forth and we were able to come up with a working plan for each picture.

Creating Your Main Character

This is often the first step in the illustration process. Share with your illustrator your ideas of how you envision your main character. The details will help make your character unique and interesting: Will it be a boy or a girl? What kind of clothes? What style hairdo? In addition to looks, what is the character's personality—carefree, boisterous, bashful? What kind of props is your character apt to be carrying—a book, a purse, a skateboard? All of this information will help in creating a unique character with an identity of its own. Your main character may be an animal. If it's a dog, what kind of dog? Again, a description of the dog's temperament and attitude will be essential. In some cases, the main character is an inanimate object, such as a car or truck. A talented illustrator will even be able to give a bulldozer the right personality!

The creation and evolution of a character: My first character was a fairy who tangles children's hair while they sleep. That's all the information I knew about her when the process began. My illustrator and I tossed ideas back and forth and decided on her personality: Aside from being happy, she would have a bit of a "hands-on-hips attitude." We then decided she should have tangled hair. Being a fairy, she should be very tiny. She travels at night, so she should be wearing pajamas. Fuzzy slippers would be a nice addition. She should be holding a lantern to help her see at night. How about carrying something, like a book titled *How To Tie Knots in Hair*? Perfect! This first step in character design was when I realized how in sync my illustrator and I were with each other, making the rest of the book creation a wonderful adventure.

How old is your character? This is an important question. In my own observation and my years of being around children as a teacher, mother and grandmother, I've noticed something interesting: Starting at about age four, children love to hang around with, and be noticed by, older children. For this reason, I prefer to have the children in my books appear to be just a bit older than my readers. However, I don't recommend this approach for baby and toddler books. Babies love to see pictures of other babies, and toddlers love to see pictures of other toddlers.

Make your characters all-inclusive. The world we live in is an ever-evolving mosaic of people with different backgrounds. For this reason, it has been important to me to include children of different ethnicities and abilities in all my books. A nice goal would be to have children everywhere feel welcome when they open your book. It also expands your audience.

The Magic Begins

Start with a storyboard. A storyboard is the illustrator's layout of the early rough drawings, drawn in pencil, visually telling the story page by page, almost like a comic book. There is one box for each page of script. This is the plan for the entire book, placing all the characters and showing their actions. It's a way to visualize what's written in the manuscript. The idea is for you now to break your text up into the corresponding spaces. You may find that you have to add more words or rearrange your thinking about what the pictures should show. You can decide where you might like a close-up drawing of a character or action. Having some close-ups, zooming in on something, adds interest to a book. At this point, realizing you need to have enough room for the pictures, you may find that you have too many words in your book. Now is the time to make any necessary changes. Remember, it's a picture book. The pictures will tell part of your story, so you don't need too many words.

On to the initial sketches. After you and your illustrator have looked over the storyboard and made the necessary corrections and additions, the next step is the initial sketches. These pencil sketches are in more detail than the storyboard and include all

An Example of a Storyboard

Illustrations © Kristi Bridgeman.

of the characters, in addition to showing the action and setting for each page. At this point, if you find that the picture and text don't quite work on a page, there is still time to rework some items. This is where you check for continuity. Are there items that you wish to add to each page? For example, if your main character is carrying a backpack, you can have it appear on each page, but in a different location. The initial sketches must also indicate where the text will go. During this process, please keep in mind that the artwork is the artist's creation; it's important to use gentle words when requiring changes at the pencil stages. Communication is key, and once you approve the artwork at each stage, you should not expect it to be changed.

Then the final sketches. At this stage the characters are refined and the details are added. You can now clearly see the characters' expressions. One of the tricky areas for the illustrator at this stage is to make certain that a character's features and proportions remain the same on each page and from every angle.

Endpapers. This is also the stage where many illustrators will create the design for the endpapers. There are four of these pages, two in the front of the book and two in the back, with one pasted against the inside of each cover. Think of the endpapers as wallpaper for your book. They can either be illustrated or left blank; however, adding a pretty endpaper gives customers a chance to see an attractive element as soon as they open the book. A small, repetitive pattern in shades of one color is always nice. These pages can also help create the color continuity throughout the book.

A color scheme is chosen. Choosing a color scheme adds a feeling of continuity as the colors flow throughout the book. This doesn't mean that these are the only colors you will see in the book, but they are colors, or shades of colors, that will be repeated in the illustrations, the cover, and the endpapers as well, making the books more unique and interesting. Keep in mind that children love bright colors.

The color is added. This is where you really see your book come alive. Some illustrators will color one page or spread at a time. Others prefer to color the important elements first, on every page that they appear. For example, the dark blue sky and the bright crescent moon might be added to each page in the book at one time. Many illustrators will email you the images as they finish each page, just to keep you calm.

The illustrations are scanned. They are now ready to be sent to the graphic designer.

The Different Stages of an Illustration

Illustrations © Kristi Bridgeman.

15. Why Do You Need a Graphic Designer?

Okay, so you have written the story and worked diligently with the illustrator to make sure your pictures match and enhance your written words. Now you have a beautiful set of pictures to go with your pages of text. Yet your project still does not resemble a book. What's the next step?

Now is the time to turn the process over to a graphic designer. Unfortunately, many authors eliminate this important step to save either time or money. They don't realize how crucial this step is to the overall quality of the finished book. Even if you or your illustrator have the computer skills to do it yourselves, you take a risk by doing so. Sometimes when the words and pictures are put together, meeting each other for the first time, there are elements that need to be added or tweaked to help them mesh. This doesn't mean there is anything missing on either end. Sometimes the parts just need a little bit of glue to hold them together and turn them into a whole. There is more to a book than just the story and some beautiful illustrations. Let's face it, you love your story, the illustrator loves the artwork—now you need someone who can objectively mesh the two elements into a book that everyone will love.

What Will the Graphic Designer Do?

Graphic designers, like editors, offer another set of eyes to look over the project. These folks are the ones who turn the separate parts of the book into a whole. They scan the original artwork, place the text on each page, coordinate the colors of the backgrounds, design the extra pages like the copyright page and title page, and "punch up" the colors of the illustrations when necessary. In most cases, your designer will also design the front cover, back cover and dust jacket. If there is a CD with your book, the graphic designer will be the one to design the artwork needed to make the CD look like an integral part of the book. He can adjust the font sizes in the book and on the cover, and even try different fonts so you can see what looks best.

Be sure to select a designer who is proficient in the Adobe Creative Suite of products. Page layout is done in Adobe InDesign, where all the artwork meets the text in one package that will then be sent to the professional print vendor. One of the best tools the designer has is Adobe Photoshop. This is where the magic really happens. A designer who is proficient in Photoshop can work wonders to modify, manipulate and fix most problems with your images, even ones that your illustrator may not be able to remedy. A designer may actually save you time and money in the long run by sidestepping the need to go back to your illustrator to redo or recreate artwork.

Perhaps best of all, your graphic designer is the person who ties up all the loose ends and presents the book to the printer in "camera ready" form. This is someone who understands the "language" of the strange-sounding names of files and downloads and will know exactly what form the book must be in before it will be accepted by the printer. With the designer speaking the same language as the print vendor, he can overcome any obstacles, hiccups or problems, such as resizing, bleed and trim specifications, spine sizes, proper resolution of images, and spacing and positioning. Since all this takes place at the very end of the project, when nerves may become a bit frayed, you will want an experienced graphic designer who knows how to cut through that stress!

How Will You Find a Graphic Designer?

As I've mentioned, when I began my journey I spent many hours doing research in libraries and bookstores and at book festivals. In addition to looking for an illustrator, I scanned the copyright pages for the words "Design and layout by..." because this is the graphic designer. Many of the ones I found, along with literally hundreds of others, have websites and can easily be contacted. You can also ask your illustrator or printer for references, and there may even be talented design students at a college near you. I was extremely lucky to have a friend, who had a friend, who knew a wonderful graphic designer. He has "performed his magic" with all five of my children's books, and now for this book.

It's important to work as closely with the designer as with the illustrator; they really *can* perform magic. For example, while working on the final illustrations in one of my fairy books, I mentioned to the designer that the hand and arm on one character looked strange in one of the illustrations. No problem. He copied and pasted an arm from the same character on another page and replaced the one I didn't like. In another of my books, there was a very blank background on one page, making it look too bare. The background was skillfully lifted from a previous page in the same book and pasted behind the characters. Magic!

So don't skimp here. This step is too crucial to eliminate.

16. Audio:
An Added Bonus

Adding audio to go along with a picture book is worth considering. It provides an added bonus for toddlers and young readers. When I started writing children's books, CDs were the most popular way to add the audio experience. Before that it was cassette tapes. Now there are other avenues to explore. You can upload digital files to your website or to various Internet resources (e.g., YouTube, iTunes and Google Play) and add a link to those files within your book. Readers can now open their books, open the files on their computer, tablet or phone, and follow along as they read. The actual audio production process, however, is the same for all.

In most cases, CDs are added to hardcover books, however I have also seen CDs in paperback books where the cover stock is sturdy enough to support the extra weight.

Why Add Audio?

It allows you to appeal to another one of the children's senses. Children learn to read by both hearing and seeing. Having a child listen to the story while following along in the book is an added advantage for beginning readers. Instead of just the flatness of words on a page, the audio narration comes alive. The story should be read with a lively voice, a bit of drama, and the emphasis on important words. This helps young readers learn the sounds and pronunciations of words and, let's face it, gives the adults a break from reading the same book over and over.

It adds a bit of independence. Children love when they can do something by themselves. Having a CD and an inexpensive CD player allows young children the freedom and independence to capture the entire reading experience. Downloadable files will also work for today's youngsters, most of whom are pretty computer savvy.

It may help with autism. Recently, at a book festival, I was approached by an excited teacher who told me of another important reason to include an audio format with a picture book. She said she was using books with audio in her teaching program with autistic children. Of course I was thrilled to hear this. After our conversation, I did some research on my own and found that many teachers and parents of autistic children agree that combining a colorful picture book with an audio format merges the best of both worlds, adding a new dimension to the learning process and making the experience more meaningful for the children. The books can now provide more of a "total experience." I'm so happy that my books are not only making children smile, but also helping them learn.

Is Creating the Audio Expensive?

While it is an added expense to produce an audio CD, it adds very little to the total printing cost and definitely adds value to the book. You may be able to recoup the money with a slight increase in the price of your book, but be careful here: Your printing cost will also depend on the size of your print run, along with a few other variables. (See the section titled "Who Will Print Your Book?") For a downloadable file, you will still have this initial production cost.

I have found a few innovative ways to save money when creating the audio format. Family and friends may hold one answer. The CD for my first book was recorded in the basement of a young audio engineer who was in the process of creating his own recording studio. He was just starting his business and was happy to get the job. Since the only room that was completely soundproof in his partially finished studio was the bathroom, parts of the recording were done while we took turns actually sitting on the toilet! I "hired" my daughter-in-law, who is a professional vocalist, to sing the song that my sister-in-law helped me write. I read the story narration. My ten grandchildren were happy to become the "children's chorus." My guitar-playing son provided the music, and—voila!—a CD was born. The nursery rhyme melodies I have used in my books are ones that are old enough to be in the public domain, making them available for public use. If you, or someone you know, have the talent to write your own melody, go for it!

For my second book, I saved money by again hiring my daughter-in-law to sing, while her friend, a former concert pianist, played the background music on a toy piano! For the third book, the sound engineer recommended a singer he had heard in a local pub. I took a group of friends with me to hear him sing and fell in love with his voice. We later learned that we do have good taste. Who would have guessed that the singer of *The Belly Button Fairy* song (Nelson Emokpae) would go on to become a contestant on the TV show *The Voice*? My main point here is that there are ways to keep the costs down and still produce a quality product. The sound engineer, though, is a must. Recording in a sound studio is the only way to give your recording a truly professional quality. Do not attempt to do it without one. It's worth every penny to do it right.

The printer normally attaches the CD to the inside front cover of the book. It's important to know that CDs need to be packaged in tamper-resistant plastic sleeves; paper sleeves are more easily broken into and, for this reason, many bookstores will not accept books with paper sleeves.

Important copyright information: According to the United States Copyright Office, songs published before 1923 are in the public domain and do not require licensing for any use. However, if they were re-copyrighted, in either the US or another country, there could still be an existing copyright. There are a number of online companies that will conduct a search of major music databases to confirm whether or not the song you choose is in the public domain. Most of the old nursery rhymes, along with their melodies, were written between 1700 and the mid-1800s and have been in the public domain for many, many years.

And Now, a (True) CD Horror Story

Once upon a time there was an author who wanted to add a CD to her soon-to-be self-published children's picture book. She thought the cost of encasing the CDs in tamper-resistant plastic sleeves was too high, opting instead for paper sleeves. They seemed sturdy enough to her. She was so confident in the quality of her book that she chose to order 5000 copies! The finished books were beautiful, so beautiful in fact that the author proudly sent a copy of the book to the head of the children's department of a very large bookstore chain. She just knew her books would be loved by all. But lo and behold, the return letter she received from this important department head stated that the books were deemed unacceptable due to the use of paper CD sleeves. To rephrase this predicament: Her 5000 books were deemed unacceptable!

Fortunately all was not lost, for you see, this author had a very large family. They loved her enough (and felt truly sorry for her) to convene on a Sunday morning around a large conference table in her son's office. Here they formed a production line and spent twelve hours unpacking each case of books, carefully removing the paper sleeves, placing each CD into its newly purchased plastic sleeve, meticulously gluing each CD back into place and repacking the books. Twelve hours later, all 5000 books were now ready to sell. The head of the children's department of the very large bookstore chain was delighted and ordered many copies of the book. The end.

The moral of this true story is twofold: Do it right the first time, and don't skimp on the important things. Also, do whatever it takes to right a wrong.

17. How to Plan the Audio Production

Kudos to you if you do decide to produce a CD or other audio production with your book. Now let's delve into the details that will help you plan this exciting adventure. Just a reminder: The recording process is the same whether your end product is a CD or a downloadable file.

Plan the Audio

Choose a recording studio. All recording studios are not the same. Make sure you choose a studio with experience in voice recording, and an engineer with experience recording the type of material you will be creating. If they have worked with narrators in the past, they will be able to offer constructive criticism about your narration and help you make any necessary corrections before the final recording is approved. Be sure to meet with the audio engineer ahead of time to work out the details and have all your questions answered. How long will your project take to record? Will they adjust the sound levels and timing, add the sound effects, delete any unwanted sounds and create the finished product? You will realize that it's not as easy as simply strolling into the studio, reading your book, and waltzing out with a finished product in your hand. If this is your first recorded book and you are going to record the book yourself, I strongly suggest that you use a professional recording studio. Yes, it will add to the cost of your project, but the expertise and insights that you gain will serve both your current and future projects and ensure that your finished project is first rate.

Plan the entire content of the recording. What else will you add to the recording? For a children's book, the story narration is the key element, but a song is always a nice addition. Soft background music is a nice touch as long as it fits the rest of the music and is not just music for music's sake. How about some interesting sound effects, like giggles, or perhaps a sound to imitate an animal in your book? It's also a good idea to have the sound of a bell as a signal each time a page should be turned. If you do choose to add this page-turning sound, the timing that I have found works best is to place it at the beginning of a three-second pause between pages to allow time for the child to turn the page. In most cases, each element of the production (song, narration, children singing, bell sound) is recorded separately, and the various components are put together at the end. There are lots of sound effects available on the Internet, and many studios have music and sound effects libraries available.

> **An example:** Each of my books includes a CD. I start each CD with about a minute of the chosen song. Then, I begin my narration with: "Best Fairy Books presents *The Knot Fairy* by Bobbie Hinman, with illustrations by Kristi Bridgeman. This is the story of a tiny fairy who visits children while they sleep and loves to tangle their hair. Now, gather 'round and get comfortable, open your book and let's begin." Following this introduction I narrate the story. And following the story, the entire song and musical accompaniment is featured. This is the basic format I have used for each recording. I end each CD with the children's chorus (my grandchildren) singing a song, reciting a few lines, or just giggling. You may think of other creative touches pertaining to your story that you would like to add.

Do your homework and be ready. This is crucial. Be sure to write your entire script before the recording session begins. This includes *every* word and *every* pause. By now you will have decided who will read the story. I firmly believe that no one can read a story with as much feeling as the author, and most people really do prefer to hear the author's voice. (When I visit schools and play the CD, the children are so excited when they realize it is my voice on the CD.) Be prepared by practicing reading your story over and over. Decide which words you would like to emphasize, and mark the notes on your script. Practice pronouncing every word. Read at a pace that is slow enough for listeners to follow along with you, but not so slow that you sound like you are about to nod off. You may have to read the story over a few times during the recording session to get it right. You will have to place your script on a stand or table in front of you during the recording session because a sensitive microphone will pick up even the tiniest sound of paper rattling. Generally, if you cough or mess up a word, you can just go back about a sentence or so and continue recording. The sound engineer will be able to combine the various takes after the recording has been completed.

Be prepared for some fine tuning at the end. This is where the audio engineer can provide the same "magic" that a graphic designer provides for illustrations. The process is a real exercise in creativity and quite a learning experience! And I can't wait to do it again!

Recording tip: A good tip to remember is to move only your eyes, up and down the page, and not to move your head. Microphones are very sensitive and, believe it or not, your voice quality can change just from moving the position of your head up and down; your voice while you are reading the top of a page may sound noticeably different from the way it sounds at the bottom of the page if you move your head. (The same holds true for side-to-side movement.) Most people don't like to hear the sound of their own voice, so try not to be overly critical of yourself. I always take my husband along because I know he will offer support and still be brutally honest.

Attractive CDs add to the overall design element of the book.

18. Pricing Your Book

It's almost time to send your book to the printer, but before you can do this, you will have to decide on the retail price so it can be added to the bar code on the back cover. This is always a stumbling block. You are naturally in love with your book and think it's the best children's book ever, but now's the time to be objective. Set a smart price so you can sell your book competitively and still make a profit.

It's time for more research. Go to your local bookstore and look at comparable children's books. What is the price for a similar book in a similar format? What you'll usually find is that the big publishing houses provide a good example of what book prices should be in order to appeal to the public. You may want to follow their lead. One of the biggest mistakes you can make is setting your price too high, which drastically reduces the likelihood that people will buy your book. On the other hand, you don't want to appear to diminish the value of your book by pricing it too low.

Find the Balance

You will need to find the balance between what you are paying to print your book and what a reasonable retail price should be. If you have self-published, the printing cost of your book will depend on the number of books in your print run; the more books you print, the lower the cost of each book. If you've used Print On Demand (POD), the printing cost per book will likely be high, so you will have to be prepared to make less money per book. Sadly, I've met too many authors who are facing this dilemma. For some, this may be the first time they realize they have paid too much to print their books. Often they price their book too high, causing it to be doomed from the start. Even printing a short run with a traditional printer will usually cost you less per book than using POD, thus enabling you to sell to bookstores at a lower cost.

If you are able to set a reasonable price for your book, but are still barely making a profit, realize that when your book sells out, you can increase your profits by printing a larger quantity next time. Keep all this in mind when choosing a printer. You don't want to be in the position of paying more for your book than you can sell it for.

Should You Factor in Your Other Book Production Costs?

No. It's true that the printing cost is not the only cost you will encounter in your publishing endeavor, but you cannot figure the others into the pricing decision. The illustrator, graphic designer and editor, for example, are one-time costs and, as such, are amortized over the life of the book. If you were to add these costs to the equation, the book would surely be too expensive to ever sell. To reiterate what I said in the previous two paragraphs: I've met too many self-published authors who are crying the blues because they felt they had to price their children's picture books at a price that proved to be much too high.

Should You Use an Even-Numbered Dollar Amount?

As consumers, we have been conditioned to think that an item marked $15.95 costs less than if it were $16.00. While we all know there is not much difference, we tend to feel that the first price I mentioned is a better buy. I personally think it's wise to do what most publishers do and price your book using the $__.95 format.

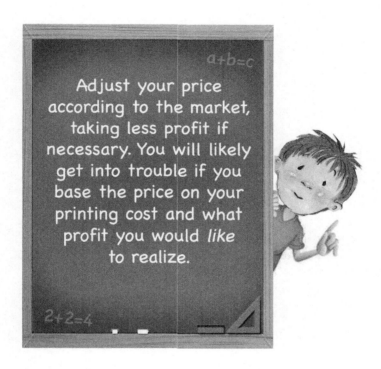

Adjust your price according to the market, taking less profit if necessary. You will likely get into trouble if you base the price on your printing cost and what profit you would *like* to realize.

19. The Dedication Goes to...

The dedication page is the place where you can honor someone special. You have worked long and hard on your book; wouldn't it be nice to dedicate it to someone who means a lot to you? Sounds easy, doesn't it? After all, it's only a few lines. I've known several authors who were able to write entire novels, yet were completely stumped when it came to the dedication page.

Who will you choose for this honor? Just stop and think a bit. Is there someone close to you who has helped you through the writing process? Is there a special person who has helped you through life? Is there someone you love, like a parent or child, or even a pet? Perhaps someone whose work has inspired you? Maybe you would like to dedicate your book to the memory of someone who was once a meaningful part of your life.

There is no form to follow and no right or wrong way to write a dedication. The most common approach is to name the person, followed by your reason for choosing them. For example: "To Sammy, for always being there when I needed a hug." It can be clever or funny if you wish, such as the one I wrote for *The Fart Fairy*: "To my precious grandchildren, who taught me to laugh at farts." Another possibility is to dedicate the book to the children who will be reading it: "For all boys and girls who believe in make-believe." Be creative. Make it simple and meaningful. Adding an illustration to the page is also a nice touch.

The placement of the dedication page is on the right hand page, opposite the copyright page.

Sample Dedication Page from The Belly Button Fairy

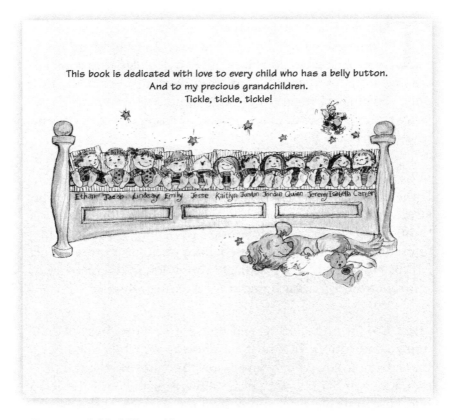

This book is dedicated with love to every child who has a belly button.
And to my precious grandchildren.
Tickle, tickle, tickle!

Ethan Jacob Lindsay Emily Jesse Kaitlyn Justin Jordan Quien Jeremy Isabella Carter

Illustrations © Mark Wayne Adams.

20. What Belongs on the Copyright Page?

The location of the copyright page is the back of the title page. This is not where you register your copyright. The necessary registration form will have to be filed with the United States Copyright Office. What you are doing on the copyright page is providing notice of the copyright.

This is the information that belongs on the copyright page:

- Title and author
- Copyright notice
- Credits
- Place of printing
- Reservation of rights
- Cataloging in Publication data
- Name and contact information of publisher
- ISBN
- Library of Congress Control Number

You can read more detailed information for obtaining the copyright, Cataloging in Publication data, ISBN and Library of Congress Control Number in the section titled "You Will Need to Apply For These..."

Sample Copyright Page from
The Knot Fairy

21. Who Will Print Your Book?

This is an exciting time. You are ready to print! But finding the right printer can seem overwhelming. This is not a last-minute decision. Your research and planning should begin at least by the time your book is in the illustration phase. This will give you plenty of time, and you will avoid a last-minute panic.

Please refer to the section titled "Alternative Methods for Self-Publishing" for information about working with Print on Demand (POD) companies.

Do Your Research

If you Google "how to find a book printer," you can have your choice of 74,300,000 listings. If you Google "book printers for self-publishers," you can choose from 2,620,000 listings. My advice is to do your own research at the same time you are researching illustrators, editors and graphic designers. For the purpose of locating printers, large book festivals are a good place to start. At these events, especially a huge one such as BookExpo (formerly known as Book Expo America, or BEA), you will find a very large selection of self-published books. This was exactly where I found my printer. I was looking not just for *nice* books, but for *exceptional* ones. I wanted my books to stand out in a crowd. At BookExpo, I did find what I considered to be some of the best-looking children's picture books. Of course, if you are not able to attend a large book event, you can still investigate the offerings at your local bookstores and libraries.

One of the great advantages of large book events is that the authors are usually on-site and willing to offer first-hand information regarding many aspects of writing and publishing. I came home from BookExpo with the names of two high-quality printers whose books I liked best, and who had been in the book publishing business for many years. Both companies happened to be in the Seattle area, and I was living in Baltimore, but with phones and the Internet, distance was not an issue. Both printers were receptive when I called and were willing to send me books and paper samples. The two quotes were about the same; however, I preferred the quality of one over the other and also found these owners to be more pleasant and accommodating. To date, this company has printed numerous editions of all five of my children's books. To summarize: Do your research!

Not All Printers Are Created Equal

As you research, you will find there are large commercial companies, small private ones and everything in-between. Some handle small jobs, while others handle more complex assignments. Many all-purpose printing companies, which have always offered newsletters, address labels and other business-related materials, are now springing into action, trying to capture the market for self-published books. Some printers have *always* specialized in books. Of these, some will print books only in paperback format; others will be able to handle the production of more complex books, such as those in hardcover format with dust jackets and audio CDs. The latter is the type of printer I would recommend, one that has been in the business long enough to be totally familiar with all aspects of book production.

As I mentioned in the section titled "Alternative Methods for Self-Publishing," the Internet is flooded with Print On Demand companies looking for self-published books. If you choose to go this route, be sure to seek a number of quotes and compare the quality, pricing and services. Make sure the books will not cost more to print than their retail price. Remember, if you want to control all aspects of your book, you *must* obtain the ISBN in your name. If you don't own the ISBN, you don't own all the rights to your book. If any printing company owns the ISBN to your book, *they* own the publishing rights.

Choices, Choices and More Choices...

Whether you have zeroed in on the printer of your choice or are still looking, there are some important decisions to be made, and a good printer will guide you through the maze. If you choose POD, you will still need to face decisions, however the choices are generally limited.

Digital or offset. Digital printing has come a long way in recent years, with the quality currently very comparable to that of traditional offset printing. The good news here is that self-publishers now have more options available, with a short run often being much more affordable than in the past. If you are considering POD, you might want to consult several printers about doing a digital short run (about 50 books or so) instead.

Paper weight. The printer can show you paper samples of varying weights. For a picture book, you will generally be offered 80 to 100# paper, the latter being heavier. For children's books, durability is an issue to consider, so I have always chosen to go with 100# stock, which is a bit more child-friendly.

Endpapers. The printer will offer you choices for the end-papers. These can be designed by your illustrator, or you can go with a solid color. If you don't specify your preference, you will most likely end up with plain white endpapers. For more information about creating endpapers, see the section titled "It's All About the Pictures! Part Three: Steps in Creating the Illustrations."

Gloss or matte. You will need to make this choice for the cover as well as the inside pages. In doing your research, take a look at both, weigh the pros and cons, and decide which you prefer. In one of my decidedly unscientific polls, among the people I asked (including both adults and children), most felt that gloss paper makes the colors appear more vivid, but agreed that it tends to show fingerprints more than matte paper. Most also felt that a matte finish looks richer and more professional, even though the illustrations don't appear as bright as those on gloss paper. (Just in case you are wondering which I prefer, it's the richness of matte.)

Hardcover. These are the most expensive to produce but also last the longest when they have to hold up to the task of being well-loved by children. Although they cost more to produce, they offer the benefit of selling for a higher price than paper-backs. Hardcover books can also include extra enhancements, such as full-color dust jackets and colorful endpapers.

Paperback. These are less expensive than hardcover books to produce, making them a popular choice. The downside is that these books will wear out faster than hardcover books. If your budget is tight, I would never recommend mortgaging your house to print a hardcover book. Instead, you might want to consider printing a quality paperback version, making it wildly successful, then revisiting the format options for your next printing.

Dust jacket. If your book is in hardcover format, you have the option to add a dust jacket. It's an additional cost that will definitely add protection and a richness in quality to your book.

If you do decide to add a dust jacket, be sure to ask your printer for a few additional ones to keep on hand in case you ever need a replacement.

Proofs and Galleys

Color proofs. These are the final unbound pages, used for checking to be sure that all text, graphics and colors are correct before going to press. Actual physical proofs are definitely necessary, enabling you to see the true color and clarity as they will appear in the finished book. By this time, all corrections should have been made. Any corrections at this point are costly, so this is *not* the time to ask to try a new color scheme or move a block of text to a different location on the page.

Galleys. Galleys are the preliminary versions of publications that can be sent to book reviewers, distributors and book clubs, who like to see a copy of the book three to six months before its official publication date. As a self-publisher, this would mean that, if you choose to send out galleys, you would then have to hold back your books for several months before releasing them. This is really not something that I recommend, for two reasons: First, you have paid for the books and are eager to start the sales process; and second, many of the reviewers who handle traditionally published books are reluctant to review self-published books. Instead of using galleys, you can wait and send finished copies of your book. This has worked for me. I send finished books, then add the reviews to my website and brochures as I receive them. In future printings, the reviews can be added to the back cover.

What Will the Printer Need From You?

Before the contract is signed and a deposit paid, the printer will most likely need to receive and review the digital files for your book. These are normally sent by the graphic designer. It's important for the designer and the printer to be in communication and work out the nitty-gritty details of file transmission. Usually the images are requested as CMYK and in 300 dpi resolution. (Your graphic designer will be able to provide this.) It's also imperative that the printer receive the files in the workable condition that he expects, avoiding any last-minute surprises on either end. The good news is that the printer will provide the graphic designer with all the necessary specifications for sizes, bleeds, resolutions, file types and delivery instructions.

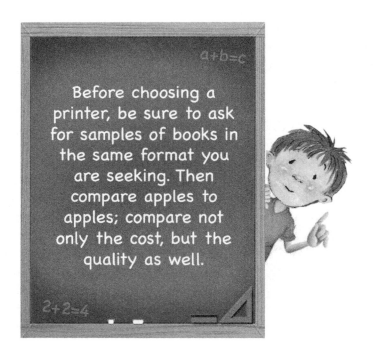

Before choosing a printer, be sure to ask for samples of books in the same format you are seeking. Then compare apples to apples; compare not only the cost, but the quality as well.

22. E-Books vs. Print Books

When I published my first picture book, there was a lot of talk in the industry about the potential demand for children's e-books, but that was still in the future. Now the future is here and it's moving fast, with new advances seemingly every day. The good news is that children's e-books are a growing market among self-published authors. The world is now our audience. But don't let this go to your head; it's also bad news. If you simply produce a mediocre e-book and sit back waiting for success to happen, guess what? Success without quality and hard work will *not* happen. You *must* produce a top-notch book and plan to market, market, market your e-book, just as you must do for your print book.

Which Format Do Customers Prefer?

Some customers prefer print books, while others prefer e-books. Still others purchase both. As an author, you can choose to produce one instead of the other, or you can create both an e-book *and* a print book. Each format has its own advantages to customers:

Advantages of print books:

- Your dollars buy you an actual book to hold in your hands.

- You get to peruse hundreds of books in bookstores, looking at the covers and examining each one to find the book that interests you.

- You get to touch and smell a real book. (Yes, book lovers will tell you how important this is.)
- You can pass the book on to a friend after you have read it.

Advantages of e-books:
- You can store hundreds of books in one easy-to-carry device.
- An e-book usually costs less than a print book.
- Shopping online is easy, and you can purchase a book with just a click.
- An e-book can be interactive, thereby adding both mental and visual stimulation.

Which Format Is Better for Children?

The e-book marketplace is growing very quickly, and this may very well be the wave of the future; however e-books can't replace snuggling on the lap of someone you love and being read to while you turn the pages of a real book. As a teacher, mother, and grandmother, I think children have a lot to gain from reading books in both formats; however, I prefer to start them with print books, then introduce e-books when they are able to read by themselves, usually in first grade. This allows for the snuggling that comes with being read to, and in no way detracts from the children's future years of becoming electronically savvy.

Good News for Authors

The good news is that, as an author, you don't necessarily have to choose between producing e-books or print books. Right now they still coexist peacefully, so you can create both if you prefer. That way you can please customers on both sides of the debate. The important thing is to get children to read more and to love it.

Which Format Should I Publish First?

I pondered this question for a while, and then talked it over with a number of my author and publisher friends. We all agreed that if you are planning to publish in both formats, a tangible book should come first. Doing it in this order gives you a certain amount of credibility that will help later in the promotion of your e-book. You will then be able to promote your e-book as a way for children to have a "traveling" version of the print book. You can also promote the notion that the e-book is now available "by popular demand."

Can I Publish Just an E-Book?

Many authors are choosing to produce e-books *instead* of print books. The bad news is that the market is swamped with e-books, and many of them are of poor quality. I say this over and over: Just as with traditional books, you *must* produce a quality e-book! If you publish a mediocre e-book, it will just sit there and get lost in the enormous crowd. You still need to have a great story, quality illustrations, an enticing cover, a good editor and a lot of marketing—at least as much as you would for a print book. If you already have a print book that isn't selling well, don't be fooled into thinking that it will automatically be successful as an e-book. It is unlikely for an e-book to come out of nowhere and suddenly turn into a bestseller. It seldom happens.

A significant downside to publishing only e-books is that this will eliminate the book signings, book festivals and other venues that offer both retail sales opportunities and personal contacts with your customers.

Will I Need an ISBN?

While an ISBN is not required by some e-book distributors, it *is* required by others. If you plan to market your e-book through multiple channels, as opposed to just Amazon (which doesn't require an ISBN), you are safer assigning an ISBN to avoid any problems later. Some e-book distribution services will provide you with an ISBN as part of the fee for their services; however, in order for you to retain full ownership and rights to your book, *you* need to purchase and assign your own ISBN. (For more information about ISBNs, see the section titled "You Will Need To Apply For These…")

Can I Publish the E-Book Myself?

Yes, you can—with a bit of help. Hand in hand with the upsurge in technology, e-book distribution companies have been popping up so quickly, it's hard to stay current. Amazon, Barnes & Noble, iBooks, Kobo and Google Play are just a few, with Amazon being the largest. Then there's Smashwords, a very large e-book distributor that distributes to Barnes & Noble, Apple iBooks, Kobo, and also to libraries via OverDrive. All of the e-book distributors offer help in converting and uploading the files and listing your book for sale. They all offer authors various free marketing tools. Compare what each one has to offer as far as ease, accessibility and advertising incentives before you make your decision; you are not limited to only one distribution channel. In addition to distributors, there are also numerous online self-publishing companies that offer to do all the work for you—for a fee. If you have published a print book and signed a contract with a distributor, be sure to read the fine print; there is most likely a clause in your contact that also gives the distributor the rights to handle the e-book distribution.

How to Price Your Children's E-Books

I am willing to bet that every e-book author feels stress over this decision. The dilemma is the same as with print books: If you price your e-book too low, will that make people think it's an inferior book? On the other hand, if you price it too high, will that put people off? A good starting point is to research other comparable e-books and their prices, while taking into account the renown of the other authors. It's wise to stay within the range of most other children's picture books. The way people perceive your book will also influence the price they are willing to pay. As with print books, the cover must be colorful and attractive, and the font legible. If the cover pops, you are likely to have a new customer.

How to Market an E-Book

Through social media. This is probably the best venue for marketing your e-book. Post announcements wherever you can, just as you would do with print books. Then follow up with future reminders. Try to tie your posts in with other book-related information so your message is not the same over and over again.

To international groups and bloggers. Join groups of e-book enthusiasts from other countries on Facebook or other social media sites. Since having to ship overseas is not an issue with e-books, you can spread your wings! I recently had a big surprise when I posted a comment on a UK Kindle group and saw one of my books already featured there!

On your website. Make sure your website is colorful and up to date, with information and links to where customers can purchase your e-book.

With free promotions. The offers by your e-book distributor to feature your e-book free for a short period of time are well worth it. Yes, *free*. These offers are among the quickest ways to generate buzz about your book.

Shortly after producing my e-books through Amazon KDP (Kindle Direct Publishing), I took part in their KDP Select program. This enabled me to offer each of my e-books free, one book at a time, one day at a time. As a result, *The Sock Fairy* became an "Amazon Bestselling Book" and I received a very nice surprise bonus along with my royalty. It's important to note that, while Amazon KDP Select has a lot to offer, it is only available if you agree to distribute your e-books exclusively through Amazon. The period of exclusivity has a time limit; currently it is 90 days, allowing you to promote through Amazon for this time period, then add other venues if you choose. Other e-book distributors also offer promotions; check the terms and conditions carefully before you join any program.

In every flyer or brochure you create. On every advertising piece you distribute, you can now boast, "Also available in digital format on Amazon and iBooks" (or wherever you have chosen to distribute).

Each online vendor has different requirements for the books they distribute. Amazon appears to be the easiest when it comes to establishing an online presence. But the market continues to evolve. Before you list your e-book, take the time to research, and then do a bit more research.

A Spike in Action on My Amazon KDP Account When I Offered a 1-Day Free E-Book

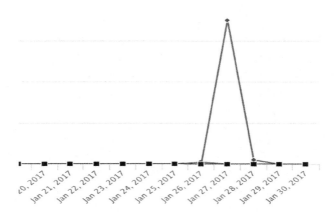

23. Distributors and Wholesalers:
Who They Are and What They Do

Knowing the difference between a distributor and a wholesaler is important, especially for writers who hope to get their books into bookstores. Basically, distributors and wholesalers provide the two main channels for getting your book into retailers like Barnes & Noble, as well as libraries and independent bookstores. You've probably heard both terms, so let's take a look at what each one means.

It's important to note that distributors and wholesalers are not interested in working with authors; they work with publishers. If authors want to have their books carried by a major distributor or wholesaler, I suggest that they start an LLC/Publishing company. An LLC, or limited liability company, shares many of the same qualities as a corporation. If you are taking on the role of publisher, you need to start here. Be sure to take the time to discuss the plans and options with a lawyer or accountant.

If your plan is simply to make your book available to your friends and family, forming a company and working with a distributor is not necessary. There are many venues for selling your book that I share with you in the last section of the book, starting with the section titled "Now on to the Marketing."

Distributors

What does a distributor do? Think of it this way: In most retail businesses, there are salespeople. Writers who are now in the publishing business can rarely afford to hire their own salespeople. Even if that were possible, a small sales force would still be unable to reach each and every bookstore. You certainly cannot even begin to undertake that impossible task. That's where the distributor comes into play. Your distributor is both your sales force and a full-service shipping company. They receive a percentage of your net sales to represent your book to the trade by selling to independent bookstores, wholesalers, big box stores, online retailers, etc. They also handle receiving and shipping stock, managing data, processing returns, and processing and invoicing orders. They are your one-stop shop to get your books into the hands of consumers.

How do you find a distributor? An Internet search will help you locate distributors that represent self-published books. Another good source is the monthly magazine published by the Independent Book Publishers Association (*IBPA Independent*). (See the section titled "Writers Associations" for more information about what this organization has to offer.) You can also ask other self-publishers for recommendations. Your goal should be to find a distributor that either works exclusively with self-publishing companies or has a small press division, and likes your book enough to accept it. It's wise to start looking before you print, but the distributors may want to wait to see your finished product before offering you a contract. It's a stretch to count on an individual book being picked up by a large distributor. However, if you have a book with steady sales, and can show that there is demand for the book, you are more likely to find a distributor willing to take you on. If you do find a small press distributor who is interested in representing your book, it's always wise to ask for—and check—a few references before you sign a contract.

Will a distributor help market your book? Absolutely! A good distributor is just as interested in selling your books as you are. Most distributors require exclusive rights to sell your book to the book trade (bookstores, libraries, department store book departments and other retail outlets that sell books). But remember that, even though the distributor will do some marketing, you, the author, are the best advocate for your book, and therefore should be constantly marketing your title to promote sales through all channels. Distributors can get your book onto the shelves at Barnes & Noble or other retailers, but you should not rely on the casual browser to discover and purchase your book. It falls on you to drive consumers to seek out your title through marketing, social media or other means. Bookstores will typically hold onto stock for 3 months, but after that, books will be returned to their distributor and charged back to the publisher.

Wholesalers

What does a wholesaler do? Think of wholesalers as the middlemen of the book industry. Ingram and Baker & Taylor are the two largest wholesalers in the United States, maintaining inventories of all active titles; this enables them to supply independent bookstores, libraries, online retailers and other accounts. Some accounts prefer to have a central book supplier, and therefore order all their books from a wholesaler rather than ordering directly from each and every publisher or distributor. While they do offer marketing opportunities such as catalogs, e-blasts or digital placement, due to the fact that a wholesaler represents every active book, they are unlikely to champion your book when doing business with their large account base.

How do you find a wholesaler? If you are a self-publishing company with fewer than ten titles, it's very difficult to have your books listed with a large wholesaler unless it is through a distributor. If you want your book in major bookstores and libraries, you will first need to find a distributor that will sell to the wholesaler on your behalf. Conclusion: You first need a distributor to have your book available through a wholesaler.

Will a wholesaler help market your book? The answer is no. It's just not what they do. The relationship with a wholesaler means having your name, title and ISBN listed in their wholesale catalog along with thousands of other titles. While it's always nice to see your name in print, just having your name in the catalog doesn't change the fact that a wholesaler alone will not get your books onto a bookstore shelf. Unfortunately for POD customers, I have met many who were promised distribution for their books, only to find that they were simply listed with Ingram and nothing more.

How Much Will a Distributor Cost?

If you are seeking professional distribution, you can plan on the distributor wanting a discount of 20 to 30 percent of net sales. Net sales equals retail price minus account discount, which is usually around 50 percent. Ouch! Although that's a big chunk of money, I always ask self-published authors this question: Would you rather keep your books piled up in storage and not make a lot of sales, or sell more books with a small profit and send them out into the world? I want my books out and in the hands of people who can share them with other people and help spread the word. I would be happy to sell a million books making only a dollar on each one! Self-publishers who have chosen POD for their printing will often find that the cost of a distributor is prohibitive when factoring in their printing cost.

In Conclusion:

Distributors offer the path to efficient distribution. As the present-day publishing industry changes and evolves, so do the services and responsibilities of distributors and wholesalers. The lines are blurring as the offerings overlap, making it even more confusing. So if processing all this information seems like a daunting task, it essentially all comes down to making the decision of whether to partner with a distributor or try to "go it alone." If your goal is to plan a marketing campaign, and you wish to see your books in major bookstores, you won't get very far without a distributor.

Bookstores prefer to order from wholesalers. Most of the orders placed by bookstores are through wholesalers rather than distributors or individual publishers, the main reason being that it is much easier to place one order through a trusted wholesaler than multiple orders through various distributors and publishers. Your path to a major wholesaler is through a distributor.

You will need to work along with your distributor. In my experience, the only efficient way to distribute books to bookstores has been through a distributor. Once you find a distributor you trust, work with them by keeping your representative up-to-date on your marketing plans. Now all you have to do is figure out how to create customer demand for your book. If you don't tell the world about your book, all the distributors in the world can't help you. (See "Part 3. The End: Look Out, World!" for lots of marketing ideas.)

Understand the contract before you sign. Before signing a contract with any book distributor, be sure to do your research. Talk to other publishers, and also bookstore managers, to help decide if the company you are interested in would be a good match for your book. Be sure you read the contract carefully and understand what services are offered, what discount they require and what role you will play in the distribution process.

Is it worth the money? If you're a self-publisher and you want to see your books in major bookstores, how else will you accomplish this feat?

Will Bookstores Ever Carry Your Books if You Don't Have a Distributor?

While the distribution system makes it difficult for most self-publishers to see their books in major bookstores, as an author you can still take your book to every bookstore within reach and present it to the manager or buyer. If you have a marketing plan in place to brag about, that will often influence their decision as to whether or not to carry your book. It is not likely that they will actually purchase the books from you; rather, they will often take the books on consignment and pay you as each book is sold. Many large bookstores also have book signings featuring only local and self-published authors. I'll throw in another reminder here: Having an outstanding cover and professionally edited book will definitely help influence the decision in your favor.

Do you know the difference between a distributor and a wholesaler?

24. What's All the Commotion About Returns?

Many first-time authors haven't heard the news about returned books. Fortunately, I had encountered the situation with my traditionally published cookbooks, so I knew what to expect when I had to deal with returns as a self-publisher. I've talked to many people in the book world about the origin of this mildly depressing situation, and the story I have heard most often is this: During the Depression, bookstores, as well as most other retailers, were having a great deal of trouble staying in business. Apparently, some publishers came up with the idea of a return system, allowing any bookseller to return any book at any time, regardless of its condition. For publishers, who were looking for a way to encourage booksellers to buy more books, this worked. It also proved to be a boost for authors because bookstores were now more willing to take a chance on unknown books. The return system is still in place today.

The sad part is that quite often booksellers will order a book and, if it doesn't sell, simply return it; then later, they may reorder the same book. So that means a book could end up being shipped to the store, then shipped back to the distributor, then shipped back to the store again. And if it doesn't sell, it gets shipped back to the distributor yet again. For this reason, the distributor does not pay authors the full amount owed to them for book sales. Rather, they hold some of the money in reserve until the next pay period, in case of returns. I am told there's been talk about changing the system for quite a while, so we'll see.

Do You Have to Accept Returns?

Yes, if you deal with a distributor, this is the arrangement they have with the major book wholesalers and retailers. Any book sent to a bookstore can come back to the distributor. So basically, until the books are in the hands of customers, they are on consignment with the retailer. For this reason, be realistic when telling your distributor to send books to a bookstore for a marketing event you have planned. If you tell them you need two hundred books, hoping to impress them, and a hundred seventy-five come back as returns, the distributor has to take them back. The bad news is that you may be responsible for all or part of the shipping costs involved, depending on your contract with the distributor. If you handle your own distribution, you will be the one taking the books back and paying the shipping costs. One of the reasons bookstores are reluctant to carry self-published books is that they need to be assured that a publisher will take back unsold books. Get used to the fact that you *will* get returns. Don't take it personally; that's the nature of the business.

What Happens to Returned Books?

Unfortunately, returned books are often damaged from being handled so many times. If I have returns that look worn, I either discount them and sell them at book fairs and farmer's markets as "gently loved" books, or I donate them to local schools or literacy groups.

Be sure to ask your tax professional if you are entitled to a tax deduction for the books you give away.

Part 3.
The End:
Look Out, World!

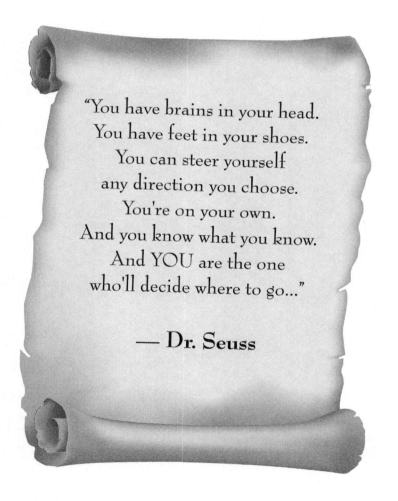

"You have brains in your head.
You have feet in your shoes.
You can steer yourself
any direction you choose.
You're on your own.
And you know what you know.
And YOU are the one
who'll decide where to go..."

— Dr. Seuss

25. Now, on to the Marketing...

Stop! Before you read on, please turn back a page and reread the quote by Dr. Seuss. Now go back and reread just the last line: "And YOU are the one who'll decide where to go..." Okay. Let's get going...

Once you have taken the plunge into self-publishing, you will have begun a long, sometimes difficult journey, one that will make you stronger and, oh, so much smarter. You will have poured your heart, your soul and your money into producing your book. Let me remind you one more time: In order to compete in the book world, you MUST produce a high-quality product! If you have done your homework and have a great book, there's no stopping now.

The thought behind my marketing strategy really comes down to a pretty simple and basic tactic: From the beginning, I have had a "let's try it" attitude. I try something, and if it works, I do it again. Simple, as long as you keep trying new things and repeating the ones that work. Marketing is forever. It goes on and on, not just for a few weeks or a few months, and not even just a few years. The promotions go on for the (hopefully long) life of the book. Some of the most important work you'll do starts long after your writing is finished. Marketing will involve a lot of focused effort, so be prepared to work at least as hard as you did producing the book in the first place. Without marketing, no one beyond your friends and family will read your book, let alone purchase it.

Marketing and Me

In this section I will share with you the methods I used to sell over 50,000 books. Some of my approaches will work for you; others may not. It's up to you to pick and choose. When I began self-publishing, the Internet was a baby. There was Facebook, Twitter, Amazon and blogging, and not too many other large social media forums. I took part in the four that I've mentioned, promoting my books as much as possible. While doing this, I also branched out by selling at book fairs and schools. This is where I made—and continue to make—the bulk of my retail sales. My distributor handles the wholesale transactions involving bookstore and library sales. I still participate in Facebook, Goodreads and a few other forums, however I often find it more lucrative to spend an entire day at a book fair than a few hours on the Internet. Although I recognize the need to do both, face-to-face sales have been my mainstay. The key is to learn to make both venues work together.

What You Will Need to Get Started

What I'm about to say may surprise you because you were probably prepared to hear me tell you to start contacting newspapers, book reviewers, bloggers, etc. That will come later. But first, you need to do more writing. Almost everyone you contact will ask you for one or more of the following:

A book description. Put together a few sentences stating the main idea of your story in a concise and appealing way that will make readers want to take a further look. An example that I have used for one of my books is: "*The Sock Fairy* is the whimsical little fairy responsible for lost socks, mismatched socks and the occasional hole in the toe." Another example is: "Her newly released book titled *Who Could Love Me More Than Scruffy?* is a story of love between a child and a rescued dog." Say as much as you can in as few words as possible.

A short bio. For advertising purposes, most people are not interested in your life story or the names of your children. They want to know who you are in relation to the world of literature. What makes you a credible writer? An example of a nice short bio might be: "Jane Doe has a B.S. degree in Elementary Education and has been teaching writing workshops for children for seven years. Her teaching experience has given her insight into the way children think and the stories they love to read." In later bios, you may be able to include, "Her previous book is the recipient of five book awards, and she has been a presenter at numerous schools, libraries and book festivals." Your bio will evolve as you add experiences to your portfolio.

When writing a bio, always refer to yourself in the third person. Also, when it comes to your education, only mention advanced degrees if relevant to your writing. For example, if you have degrees in business or accounting, and you have written a children's fairy tale, it might be better to mention other more relevant credentials.

A professional photo. This means a headshot, and it doesn't mean a selfie, although I must admit, I've tried. It needs to be a high-resolution photo and you should be dressed casually, but not sloppily.

Testimonials. Start collecting testimonials about you and your books, and keep a list. As you receive reviews, add them to your list. This means credible blurbs and reviews from well-known people, reviewers, and magazine or newspaper articles.

Your all-important book cover. Most reviewers and interviewers will ask for a high-resolution copy of your book cover. This can be provided to you by your cover designer. You will use this over and over and over again—in all of your marketing and in anything you do that involves your book. In fact, this will actually be asked for more than the photo of yourself.

The publication date. People you contact ahead of your release will want to know the publication date of your book. This refers to the date you are actually going to have the book available for purchase. It does not mean the date the book went to the printer, the date you filed for the copyright or any other random date.

The Very Big Question

Stop! Here it is again—the same question I posed before:

What Makes My Book Unique?

What is YOUR answer to the BIG question?

Now is the time to make a list of the features that make your book unique. Try to come up with at least four! Then use this information to brag and blog about your upcoming book. Post it on your social media sites and feature it on your website. Share it with bookstores, libraries, book reviewers and anyone who will listen.

The journey has begun…

26. Create a Marketing Plan

D on't let the words "marketing plan" scare you. Think of the plan as your guide to getting the books into the hands of your audience. If you plan carefully, you will be able to make the most of your time, money and hard work, and your marketing plan will guide you through the process. It doesn't have to be fancy; a single sheet of paper will do. Just remember, you can't get where you're going if you don't know where you are planning to go. So let's begin.

Know your target audience. Zero in on your audience. You will want to target your marketing as directly as possible to your potential readers. Who are they? I've mentioned a number of times how important it is to know your audience, and now it's time to put it in writing. Your list may look something like this:

- Children ages 3 to 7 years
- Parents and grandparents of children ages 3 to 7 years
- Bookstores
- Libraries
- Elementary schools and preschools

Set your goals. What are your actual goals? Decide what you realistically want to accomplish in the next year. Think about where you will have the best sales opportunities for your book.

Do you want to seek reviews? Do you want to generate media attention? How will you spread the word about your book? Your list may look something like this:

- Organize book signings
- Advertise through a social media campaign
- Build a website
- Exhibit at book fairs
- Visit schools and libraries
- Enter book award contests
- Identify niche market opportunities for book sales
- Set up interviews on podcasts
- Send press releases

Plan your actions. Now it's time to list your concrete plan of action to meet those goals. Who will you actually contact? Which bookstores? Which schools? What award contests will you enter? Your list may look something like this:

- Start a social media campaign:
  - Blog twice a week
  - Actively promote twice a week on Facebook, Twitter and Google+
- Register a domain name and design a website
- Contact area bookstores; arrange meetings with store managers to set up book signings
- Visit local libraries to set up story time visits for children
- Call local preschools to set up meetings with coordinators to schedule school visits
- Register to be an exhibitor at two or three book fairs
- Identify and enter three book award contests

- Create a press release and send it to local newspapers and magazines
- Contact regional radio stations for interviews

Establish your budget. Create a realistic budget based on your lists above. Make a list of the marketing materials you would like to purchase and the book fairs and book award contests you would like to enter. Do the necessary research and write the actual cost next to each item. Choose which items you can purchase right way, and make an additional list of the items you hope to purchase the following month. The list may look something like this (current estimates):

Purchase now:

- Website design and domain name (varies according to the different companies and plans)
- Marketing materials:
    - 250 bookmarks............................$35
    - 50 school brochures...................... $40
    - 250 postcards.............................$35
- Mailing supplies:
    - 50 padded mailing envelopes.......... $45
    - 200 mailing labels.......................$28

Next month:

- Booth supplies:
    - table cover................................$22
    - banner....................................$40
- Giveaways for customers:
    - 250 plastic dogs (or whatever fits the theme of your book)............................ $4.75/dozen

Tailor the marketing plan to *your* needs and budget. You may have fewer items on your list than I've suggested; you may have more. Only *your* goals and budget matter. Look over your list and make adjustments every month during the first year. If the list needs to be altered, that's fine. Don't feel like you've failed if you haven't accomplished everything on the list.

Note: The printing prices quoted above are approximate and are based on pricing from vistaprint.com and uprinting.com, both of which I have used consistently. The prices do not factor in the frequent sales often offered. The toy prices are based on pricing from orientaltrading.com and rinovelty.com, both of which I have used for purchasing inexpensive giveaways. The actual prices will depend on a number of variables, including the size and quantities of the items ordered.

27. Write a Press Release

Warning: It's going to take a LOT of words for me to tell you how to write a simple, one-page press release that uses as few words as possible! So pour a cup of coffee (or wine), sit back, and here we go:

A press release is a written statement to the media announcing news items. You can either hire a public relations firm to write one for you, or you can do it yourself. Guess which way I do it? You've probably guessed right. With some online companies advertising that they will send out up to 1,000 press releases for you, at a high cost of course, one can only imagine how inundated media personnel must be. I've actually often wondered if, amidst the piles of other incoming press releases, a release sent by an individual author is perhaps noticed more than one sent by a PR person. If you write and distribute the press release yourself, this may prove to be an inexpensive form of publicity with far-reaching benefits, so it's worth trying. I go for free advertising rather than paid advertising whenever I can.

When to send a press release. One ideal time to send a press release is when you are launching a new book. Later you can send other releases when you are scheduled to be a guest presenter at a book event, are doing something great for a charity, have received an award, or have any other newsworthy happenings to report. If you are announcing a new book, be certain it is available for purchase before you let the press know. If you are working with a distributor, make sure they have the books in stock, and let them know you are sending the press release. If you are handling your own distribution, be sure your website is up to date and ready to handle the sales.

Keep it short and sweet. Your goal is to say as much as you can about your book in as few words as possible. Remove any fluffy words like *beautiful, special, unique* and *wonderful*, and get to the basics. Think about what it is that makes your book stand out. What sets it apart from other books? Stick to one page, which is the norm. Two pages are acceptable, but dangerous because of the tendency to get carried away with too many words and glowing remarks about yourself and your book. It is also okay to show a sense of humor in your writing, as long as you keep it short and avoid being corny.

Make it grammatically perfect. I can't stress this enough. This is a crucial piece of advertising, and there's no room here for a misspelled or misused word, or a grammatical error. This press release represents you, so triple-check before sending it.

Write in third person. Press releases are always written in third person. Don't use "I" or "we" unless you're using it in a quote.

Format. Keep the paragraphs and sentences short and to the point. The font should be clear and readable, such as Helvetica, and the size of the type should be 12-point. Use standard letter size paper and standard business size envelopes. Press releases can be either double-spaced or single-spaced; if you choose single spacing, still use double spacing between paragraphs. Also, if you are a lover of exclamation marks, be aware that journalists frown on their use in press releases.

The Parts of a Press Release

There are many variations of the basic press release format. Following is the one I have always used:

At the top of the page. At the top of your release, in bold capital letters, you should type "FOR IMMEDIATE RELEASE" or "FOR RELEASE: (DATE)."

Contact information. This information is generally at the top of the press release. Journalists know to look for it there, and moving it to another location would mean they might have to hunt for it. Include your name, phone, fax and email. Also include the name of your contact person if you are lucky enough to have someone assisting you.

Headline. This is where you grab the readers' attention and give them a reason to want to learn more about your book. It also offers the journalist a first impression of you and your work, thus making it the most important part of the press release. If you don't grab their attention here, there's a chance they may not read any further. Make the headline short, amusing, to-the-point and creative. Phrasing it in the form of a question can also be catchy. The headline should be in bold capital letters.

Introduction. Start with your city, state and the date you are sending the press release. Then entice the reader by writing a compelling first paragraph that sums up your story in about fifty words. The job of this paragraph is to make your book or event sound exciting. Only the most important information should be in this paragraph. I'll admit, this takes some thought!

Main body paragraph. In this paragraph, you will give some background information about your book. Make it short and direct, rather than long and "fluffy." This can include the location or backdrop of the story, if relevant; it can also include details, such as the type of illustrations, the addition of an audio CD, or the fact that it is a rhyming story. Be sure to mention the features and benefits that make your book unique. Keep in mind that your goal in the press release is to inform, not promote.

About the author. In this paragraph you will need to mention your own qualifications to write the book. This is where you can mention previous awards and other books you have written. If this is your first book, you might say something like: "Jane Doe has a degree in Early Childhood Education and has been teaching kindergarten for ten years."

Summary. Give a very brief wrap-up of your book or event, or, if you have written other books, tell what types of books you produce. Now is the time to mention who your targeted customers are and where people can go for more information about you and your book.

The end. Below the summary, on the left-hand side, write: "To place an order, or arrange a book signing or interview: (your name, company name, phone, fax, email and website URL)."

At the very end of a press release, type ### in the center of the page. This signifies the end of the release and indicates there are no other pages.

How to Send It

Email. Email is an accepted method of sending press releases. First type the headline of the press release in the subject line of the email. Then copy and paste your press release into the body of the email. Don't add any attachments, or your email is sure to meet its end in a spam folder.

Sending your emails one by one is time consuming, but highly recommended. If you are sending emails in groups, DO NOT put your entire media list in the "To:" field; if you do, the recipients will each receive an email that includes the email addresses of everyone else you are sending it to. Here's what to do instead: Take a group of email addresses, separate each with a comma, and paste the group into the blind carbon copy (Bcc) field of your email message. This will prevent the multiple recipients from seeing who else received the message. Put only your own email address in the "To:" field of the group email. Send the email to just a few people at a time to minimize the risk that the message will be blocked by a spam filter. It's also a good idea to first send one email to yourself as a test, just to check the format and be sure you are happy with the way it looks.

Snail mail. I've recently spoken to several authors who felt that, with many journalists these days receiving tons and tons of press releases by email, it might be better to go back to sending press releases through snail mail. I think it also looks a bit more professional and shows that you felt it was worth the time— and the stamp.

When to Send It

Press releases should be sent a minimum of three weeks in advance, especially if you are announcing special events or holiday promotions. This gives the reporter enough time to write the story and do any research he or she may feel is necessary. Monthly publications usually need the information two months in advance of the issue date.

Send It to...

When contacting publications, keep in mind that it's proper press release etiquette to send your release only to one person at each news outlet.

Look for publications that reach your audience. Find appropriate publications. If you have a children's book, there's no point in sending your press release to the *Wall Street Journal* or *Popular Mechanics* magazine. Look through the publications you think might be interested, and try to identify editors or reporters who you think may take the most interest in you and your book.

Your local paper. Let your local media know that there is an author in their midst. Contact the city editor or the editor in charge of the section that relates to children or books. It generally isn't necessary to send press releases all over the country unless you are a well-known author, or the topic of your book relates in any way to a specific location. If you live in Florida, you are not likely to get coverage from an Illinois newspaper. However, it is likely that your local media will want to write about you and your book just because you live in that area. Be sure to mention your local ties in the press release.

Online newspapers. When sending press releases by email, be sure the editors and reporters accept press releases via email. It may take a phone call to check before sending.

Bloggers. There are so many bloggers out there who would love to hear from you. Look for those who write about children, parenting, toddlers, children's books, reading, rhymes, etc. Then look for those who write about topics specific to your book, such as fairies, kittens, trucks, etc. Send each one an email with one or two sentences about your book, and ask if he or she would be interested in receiving your press release and considering you as a guest blogger on their site.

Your website. It's a good idea to have a page on your website titled "Media," where you can keep your latest press release available for download.

Social media. You can post a link to your press release on any social media site.

Radio and TV stations. Generally the contacts for radio and TV stations are the news director or news department. A phone call is always advisable before sending a press release.

Sample Press Release

FOR IMMEDIATE RELEASE

Bobbie Hinman
Phone: xxx-xxx-xxxx
Fax - xxx-xxx-xxxx
Email: fairybooklady@bestfairybooks.com

THE FRECKLE FAIRY IS COMING! FIRST STOP: HARFORD COUNTY

Hey Kids. Do *you* have freckles? Where did they come from? Did you ever think of blaming it on a fairy?

BEL AIR, MD - October 1, 2016 - Award-winning author Bobbie Hinman will be answering these questions when she visits Bel Air this month to launch her new book, *The Freckle Fairy*. Her young fans have been eagerly awaiting this fifth book in Bobbie's fairy series. She chose her hometown for the launch, saying she would never consider launching her new book anywhere but in Harford County.

The Freckle Fairy is a rhyming picture book, accompanied by an audio CD of the story narration and an original fairy song. It features original watercolor illustrations throughout, and a simple premise: Who better to blame it on than a fairy? The Freckle Fairy follows Bobbie's other books: *The Knot Fairy, The Sock Fairy, The Belly Button Fairy* and *The Fart Fairy*. Together the books have received a total of twenty-four children's book awards.

Bobbie has a B.S. degree in Elementary Education from Towson University and is a former teacher. She loves to create stories that reveal some of the less practical and more magical explanations for life's troublesome dilemmas. Bobbie has been a speaker and presenter at numerous schools, libraries and bookstores, as well as major book festivals, all across the United States and in Canada.

The launch party will be held at the Bel Air Barnes & Noble location on Saturday, October 29th at 11:30 am. Bobbie will be there (wings and all) to read *The Freckle Fairy* and sign all of her fairy books. There will be gifts, prizes, face painting, story time and delicious treats. Kids can even come in costume if they wish.

ISBN 978-0-9786791-2-5

To place an order, or arrange a book signing or interview:
Bobbie Hinman
Best Fairy Books
Phone: xxx-xxx-xxxx
Fax: xxx-xxx-xxxx
Email: fairybooklady@bestfairybooks.com
www.bestfairybooks.com

###

28. Create a Sell Sheet

It's a good idea to create a sell sheet for your new book. This is a one-page flyer containing all the important details of your book. In fact, this is the first place you can actually use the information you carefully compiled in the earlier section of this book, titled "Now On To The Marketing..." The sell sheet is a promotional piece that you can use to share the information about your book with retailers in a quick, easy-to-read format. It's a way to present your book to the public on one sheet of paper. If you are *not* represented by a distributor, you can use a sell sheet to promote your book to independent bookstores. Also reach out to niche market retailers, such as children's clothing stores and gift shops. Think of it as an announcement of your book and where it is available for purchase. Is a sell sheet mandatory? No, but it's one of the easier forms of marketing.

Even if you have a distributor, you can create your own sell sheet to use as a promotional tool to supplement their marketing efforts. A member of their team will likely create a sell sheet for their use when marketing your book to bookstores, libraries and their other retail outlets. Be sure to include the distributor's contact information on your sell sheet and direct any pertinent purchase inquiries to their sales department.

A sell sheet typically includes:
• Book title
• Book cover photo
• Author bio

- Book description
- Publisher
- Target age group
- ISBN
- Book format and dimensions
- Distributor or places where the book is available
- Publication date
- Price

It may also include:
- Author photo
- Marketing and publicity plans
- Testimonials or reviews
- Book awards

This looks like a lot of information to cram onto one 8.5x11-inch sheet of paper, but it can be done if you choose readable fonts and keep it simple. Use as few words as possible to get your message across. Remember, this sheet has a purpose—to capture the interest of buyers. Make it attractive, but avoid going overboard with frilly decorations. If possible, use color and design that tie into the theme of your book. For a professional appearance, choose quality paper with a gloss finish. If you print your sell sheets on your home printer, invest in a pack of high-end paper. You can also check the many online printing companies that have ready-made design templates for you to follow. Remember to watch for their sales, but don't stock up on too many sheets at a time. As you receive awards and/or reviews, or release another new book, you will want to update your sell sheet.

You can distribute your sell sheets either as an email attachment or through the mail. I prefer the latter; the recipient then has an actual copy to hold onto and perhaps show to other employees. The important thing is to distribute your sell sheets freely!

Sample Sell Sheet

The Freckle Fairy
Who better to blame it on
than a fairy?

Book and Audio CD

By Bobbie Hinman

In this rhyming story, a whimsical little fairy flies through the sky at night and kisses children while they sleep. For every kiss, a freckle magically appears.

Best Fairy Books
Publication Date: September 2016
ISBN: 9780978679125
Hardcover with dust jacket
8.5x11 inches
Price: $16.95
Ages 3-7

Distribution by Midpoint Trade
www.midpointtrade.com

ABOUT THE AUTHOR: Bobbie Hinman has a B.S. degree in Elementary Education. Thanks to her teaching experience and her ten grandchildren, she is right at home in the world of children's literature. Bobbie loves to create stories that reveal some of the less practical and more magical explanations for life's little mysteries. The first four books in the fairy series are the recipients of numerous children's book awards.

www.bestfairybooks.com

Also by Bobbie Hinman:

9780978679101   9780978679118   9780978679132   9780978679149

29. Blast Off With a Book Launch Party

Your new book is being released and you want the world to know. You are excited, and you want to have a party to celebrate the launch. Do you simply throw a party and hope people show up? Let's see—there's your sister and her husband. Surely they will come. Mom and Dad are in. Your friends from the gym will certainly support you... Or, would you rather have a *real* event? Is it possible to have 100, 200, even 300 people attend your party? The answer is a resounding yes. It all starts with organizing the details of the event and putting aside your fears that no one will come. This can be an expensive event, but if you budget creatively you can do a lot of the work yourself. Keep in mind that it's a one-time event in the life of your book. Below, in detail, are suggestions to make your book launch party a success. This is the plan I followed with each of my books. There were 100 people at my first launch, with the numbers climbing as I got better at planning. My last book launch party drew over 300 people! This is my plan:

Countdown—Four Months Ahead

Decide on the time and place for your party. A local bookstore is my first choice for this type of event. You will ideally have already visited the store and introduced yourself, setting the stage for a mutually rewarding long-term relationship. Your book may still be in the printing stage, so when you meet the management team for the first time, take along your illustrations or proofs to show them how appealing your book will look. If this is not your first book, also take your other books along to show them. Tell the team about yourself and how hard you will work to make the event special. Remember, this is not only *your* party—it's also the store's event. The planning process will involve a lot of contact with the store management: Be sure to always be friendly and wear a smile so they will be happy to see you.

Plan the event thoroughly. Meet with the store manager and plan every detail. What will be the attention-getting theme for the party? Will there be decorations? What is the best day and time for the event? What will the store employees be available to help you with on that day? What will *you* provide? Will you be reading your book? Will you read more than one book? Is there a microphone available? Will refreshments be served? What handouts will be offered?

Plan your media advertising campaign. Make a list of the newspapers and news magazines in your area. Add to that list the names of any other local publications that feature event calendars or may be interested in writing an article about you or your book. Many communities have small magazines featuring local news and advertising, which are distributed to businesses and doctors' offices. Locate websites and blogs that pertain to children's books. Make a detailed checklist of all this information.

Plan your local promotion. Take note! This is a vital step that will potentially attract most of your attendees. Make a list of all the establishments in your area that may allow you to place your flyers or invitations. This could include daycare centers, preschools and libraries. You may also want to approach kinder-garten teachers or scout troop leaders. For the most part, choose locations that relate to children; however, it is often helpful to also target places where moms and grandmas congregate, such as beauty shops, gyms, coffee shops, etc. Don't forget children's stores, toy stores and senior centers. I have even left invitations in several doctors' offices (with permission, of course). Call or visit each business and, in your most professional manner, ask the managers if they would be willing to distribute invitations to their clients for an upcoming book event at the local bookstore. For schools and daycares, ask for an approximate count of the number of children who will be receiving the information. It helps to mention that one of the goals of the program is to encourage children to read. Be careful not to come across as simply wanting their help in selling more of your books.

Add a guest. You can attract more people to the event by having your illustrator attend to demonstrate sketching techniques. People love the idea of having multiple autographs in their books. If you have a CD in your book, inviting the vocalist to perform is always an added bonus. Be sure to include this essential information in your advertising/promotion.

Countdown—Three Months Ahead

Contact the media, websites and blogs on your list. Now is the time to go through your media checklist and set up your online interviews. Be sure to make a list of the dates that each one would like to receive your press information, namely the press release, bio, book summary, cover image and photo. Let each of the contacts know if you are able to offer pre-release copies of your book.

Countdown—Two Months Ahead

Have postcards/invitations printed. Postcards printed in full color on glossy stock look very professional and make ideal invitations. These can be ordered from a number of online printing companies and are sometimes less expensive than the typical humdrum black-and-white flyers. If you're up for the challenge, order at least 1,000 to 1,500 invitations, but only if you know that your goal will be to have each and every invitation find its way into the hands of a potential buyer. Check the printing websites carefully so you can save money by taking advantage of their sales and promotions. Be sure to make your event sound enticing. The promise of a gift, refreshments, or a raffle for a free book will add allure to your event. For children's books, invite children to come dressed as one of the characters in your book. Find an artistic teenager to do face painting. Make it clear on your invitations that this is a party, a happening!

Plan a poster for the store. Normally, large bookstores will provide the posters to promote your event. I always ask if they would like me to provide several additional 8.5x11-inch flyers for the window. These are easy to print at home. Flyers should include a copy of the book cover, along with the date and time of the event. Ask the store manager to display your book in the window next to your flyer.

Purchase the giveaway items. Plan to feature something special, and give something away. Scour the dollar stores and the many websites that carry inexpensive gift items. If you would like to splurge, you can have plastic cups imprinted with your logo. These can be handed out empty, or you can fill them with goodies, such as a small notepad, a candy bar, a small toy, and so forth. Magnets imprinted with your logo are another gift that will keep your name in front of your audience. Be creative and look for inexpensive items that are related to your book. Always be sure to keep in mind the age of your audience and not hand out anything sharp or too easy to swallow.

Countdown—One Month Ahead

Check with the hosting store manager. While it is important to keep in touch with the store manager throughout the entire planning process, now is the time to make sure they have ordered your books. It's also helpful to formulate a backup plan in case the books sell out during the event. This may sound like wishful thinking, however it does happen. Often the store manager will want you to have an additional supply of books in your car "just in case."

Review your media and blog lists. Send the information that has been requested. This is also the time to start promoting your event on Facebook, Twitter and any other social networking sites. (Then add a reminder every week and also on the day before the party.) This is a good time to invite your friends and family; follow up with an email requesting that they forward it to *their* friends and family.

Ask for help. Enlist a reliable friend or two to assist you at the event. It's a comfort to have someone there to help distribute the gifts, serve the refreshments, and (hopefully) run to your car each time the bookstore needs additional books. Schedule your face painter, and perhaps some of her friends, to help with a craft or distribute coloring pages related to your book.

Begin distributing your invitations. Deliver about 200 invitations to the bookstore and assist the staff by arranging them near the information counter and at the checkout registers. Speak with the store manager about having an invitation placed in the bag along with each purchase. Stop by the store every few days to replace the invitations as necessary; however, don't overload them with too many at one time. This is also a good time to deliver invitations to local libraries.

Countdown—Three Weeks Ahead

Distribute more invitations. Review the list you made months ago of target locations, and get to work. Remember, the goal is to place the invitations where they are most likely to make it into the hands of potential buyers.

Make sure the bookstore has received its order of books. This is important if the books are coming from a distributor. If you are supplying the books, now is the time to deliver them to the store. Don't forget: If you have written other books, it's also important to have these titles on hand for purchase at the event. This is especially true if your new book is part of a series.

Countdown—Two Weeks Ahead

It's time to distribute the remaining invitations. Yes, every one of them! This is a good time to deliver cards to the daycare centers' and schools. Be sure to talk to people in the grocery checkout line and hand each one an invitation. If you have an email list, be diligent about sending an email invitation to everyone you know, requesting that they forward the email to everyone *they* know. Send or personally deliver an invitation to your local news media. Oh yes, and don't forget to remind your friends and family.

Order the refreshments. If you are having a cake or special cookies made for the event, now is the time to place the order. Many grocery stores and bakeries make delicious, affordable cakes. I have always ordered a large sheet cake and had it decorated with my book cover image. Now is also the time to ask a friend or family member if they will be there to cut and hand out cake. Of course, you must check with the bookstore management first before you plan to serve food.

Countdown—One Week Ahead

Distribute any remaining invitations. Yes, the ones you are holding onto! They are of no use to you after the party. Remind all of your social networking friends of the event.

Check your lists. If you have done everything on your list, you are nearing the finish line. If not, get to work!

Launch Time—The Day of the Event

Arrive one hour ahead of the crowd. Bring a bright, attractive table cover, several pens, the refreshments, the giveaways and any props you might need. Some balloons are always a festive touch. Also bring your close friend, or friends, for assistance and moral support. Dress nicely. If you can, wear something a bit gimmicky that reflects a character in your book. I always wear a sparkly fairy dress and wings to my events. Be sure to wear your smile and treat the store personnel with respect. This is their event too, so don't act like a prima donna.

Yes, it's very hard work. And it takes a lot of planning. However, it works! The launch parties for my books have resulted in the sale of 200+ copies of each new book, along with approximately 50 copies of each of my previous books. (Well worth having writer's cramp the next day.) In addition, bear in mind that the effects of your promotions will be felt not only the day of the event, but for days, weeks, and even months to come.

Think of the movie line, "If you build it, they will come." Now remember this version: "If you plan it well, they will come!"

This section first appeared in 2010 as an article in the *IBPA Independent*, the monthly magazine of the Independent Book Publishers Association. I still follow the same plan.

Sample of a Book Launch Party Invitation

Front

You're Invited To A Party!

Back

Celebrate with us as we launch *The Fart Fairy*!
Author Bobbie Hinman will be reading& signing her newest book. Bobbie is
also the author of the award-winning books, *The Knot Fairy, The Sock Fairy* &
The Belly Button Fairy.

Meet Mark Adams, illustrator of *The Fart Fairy*.
A former Disney artist, Mark will be demonstrating his fairy illustration
techniques. Enter a drawing to win one of his sketches.

Also featuring live music by "Uncle Pete." His upbeat musical performances
have made him a favorite among school children and parents alike.
"Uncle Pete" is featured on the CD that accompanies *The Fart Fairy* book.

Location: Barnes & Noble ~ Bel Air, MD
Date: Saturday, June 5th ~ ~ Time: 11 AM
(Pre-orders for The Fart Fairy are now being accepted at the store.)

The Fart Fairy is the mischievous little fairy we love to blame for the
mysterious sounds and odors that are a part of everyday life.
Book includes an audio CD with words and music.

Storytime ~ Prizes ~ Face Painting ~ Gifts ~ Crafts ~ Cake

Fairy costumes are welcome!
For information, please call 410-638-7023
www.bestfairybooks.com
Free whoopee cushion with the purchase of a book!

Created on Vistaprint.com.

30. All About Book Signings
Part One: The Perfect Book Signing—A Fairy Tale

Once upon a time, in an urban kingdom far, far away, lived a talented author. This talented author had written a wonderful book, full of fanciful illustrations, a book that she knew would be loved by children all over the land.

One day this author was called on her magical cellphone by the manager of a large bookstore in the bustling center of the kingdom. The manager asked the author if she would like to come to the bookstore to read her book to the children of the kingdom, and to autograph it, too. The excited author jumped up and down and shouted with glee. All her life she had wanted to write books and now—a book signing!

The bookstore manager made all the plans. She called the *Kingdom Herald*, the largest newspaper in the land, and told them of the event, making sure the details were all correct. She posted the information on the store's website. She also posted large signs both inside and outside the bookstore. She even had flyers printed and handed them out to all the people in the land, telling them of the coming event.

On the day of the event, the sun was shining brightly in the sky. The bookstore manager sent a horse and carriage to pick up the author. When she arrived at the store, the author was thrilled to see a large, colorful poster on the front door announcing the book signing. A store employee greeted the author and helped her carry her belongings into the store. The author was delighted to see a large pile of her books, beautifully displayed, right in the front of the store where everyone could see them. A table and comfortable chair, placed in the busiest spot in the store, were ready for her. People were already in line, waiting patiently to purchase their books, happy smiles on their faces. Eager children were joyfully grasping their copies of the book in their clean little hands. Each adult had even been handed a post-it note on which to write the long list of names of the people for whom they were buying books. By the end of the day, everyone in the kingdom would own their own copy of the author's book.

All went well that day. When the author was thirsty, a bottle of water was handed to her. The manager asked several times if there was anything she could do to make sure the author was comfortable and the event was running smoothly. Many books were sold that day. So many, in fact, that the bookstore manager had to run swiftly to her telephone and order more books that very day.

At the end of the day, everyone was smiling. It had been a very happy day in this large bookstore in the bustling center of the kingdom. The manager thanked the author for taking time out of her busy schedule to spend time at the bookstore. One of the store employees helped the smiling author carry her belongings back to the waiting carriage. While bidding her farewell, the manager told the author to be sure to come back soon. All was well! This had been a perfect book signing. The end.

This is a fictional story. Any similarities between this story and real life are totally and completely coincidental.

30. All About Book Signings
Part Two: The Perfect Book Signing—The Reality

I hope you enjoyed reading my little fairy tale. Now back to the real world. Book signings are dreaded by many authors, yet loved by others. For some, book signings are a lifetime dream. So much depends on how you, the author, approach these events. I have had the pleasure of attending many, many book signings. Every bit of my advice comes from my actual experiences, and much of the information also holds true for exhibiting at book fairs. Keep in mind that book signings are only one piece of the marketing puzzle; they are not the only option for promoting your books. Unless your book is already wildly popular, without a serious marketing effort, it's unlikely your signing will attract many people.

How to Schedule a Book Signing

A local bookstore is an ideal first choice for scheduling a book signing. The first step can be done either before your book is released, or with an existing book. Start with a visit to the store (or stores) and introduce yourself to the manager and/or community relations coordinator. Tell them a little about yourself, being sure to mention any credentials that add to your credibility as a writer. It's important to make the first connection in person, rather than by email.

If your book is already in print, be sure to bring it with you; simply talking about it is meaningless. Also bring a copy of your sell sheet, a school brochure, copies of important reviews and awards, or any similar examples of your marketing skills.

Even if a book signing is not scheduled for you during this meeting, it's wise to leave all the information with the manager, *including* a copy of the book. They now have a friendly reminder for future signing possibilities. You can drop by a few weeks later and let them know about a new marketing campaign you are implementing, an award your book has received, etc.

If your book has not yet been released, bring along a copy of the cover or some illustration samples. Later, when your book is ready, make an appointment to visit the store to show off the finished product. Bring along a copy of the sell sheet you have created and the press release you are planning to send to the local newspaper announcing the arrival of your new book. (See the sections titled "Create a Sell Sheet" and "Write a Press Release.") In both cases, if you have done your homework, and your book was professionally illustrated and edited, you have an excellent chance of scheduling a signing.

Grouchy Authors Not Allowed!

Now, my rant: It never ceases to amaze me how disagreeable and unapproachable some authors appear! At one recent event, I was tempted to grab my camera and take a few pictures to demonstrate the *don'ts* of author behavior; I must admit that the fear of a lawsuit kept me sane. Why do so many authors stack their books in neat piles on the table and proceed to sit behind the piles wearing deep frowns on their faces? Their expressions say loud and clear, "Don't dare speak to me!" I recently witnessed one author who was silently reading a book, another playing a game on a cell phone, and another—in my opinion the worst one of all—typing away on a laptop. All this was done while they were supposedly introducing their books to the public. Is this really the image you wish to portray? Not surprisingly, these are the same authors who grumble at the end of the day about their poor book sales. Rant over!

What I Learned in the Trenches

On the more positive side, now that my rant is over, here is some valuable information that I have learned along the way:

Work out the details ahead of time. It's a good idea to meet directly with the people who will be in charge of setting up and running your signing. Make sure they have the information necessary for ordering the books (from your distributor or wholesaler, or from you, only if you handle your own distribution). A subsequent call about two weeks before the signing is a good idea, to make sure the books have been ordered.

Many book signings begin with a reading of the book, followed by the actual signing. If this is the case, take a look at the space you will be using and determine what you will need. Electricity? A microphone? It helps to have the arrangements in place before the big day.

Ask what you can do to help. Find out what the store employees will be doing to promote the signing, and ask what you can do to help. One way is to offer to print flyers to be handed out in the store before the event. I have found most store personnel to be happy to receive these. The ideal size is half of an 8.5x11-inch sheet of paper. Simply design the flyers with two on each sheet, then cut the sheet in half. You can cut costs further by printing in black ink on a brightly colored paper, rather than printing in full color. In addition, you can offer to print an 8.5x11-inch flyer for the store's front door or window. You can assist with promotion by spreading the word to all your friends, *their* friends and your social media friends, by posting on your website, and by contacting your local newspapers. Read through my marketing ideas in the section titled "Blast Off With a Book Launch Party," and apply any ideas that will work here to attract customers.

Check your expectations at the door. Whatever your expectations, leave them home. Every book signing is different. Some draw huge crowds, while others may only have five people attend. Don't let the size of the crowd affect you. The purpose of a book signing isn't only to sell your books. It's also to sell yourself. The entire time you are there, your name is in front of the reading public. Bear in mind that so is your face, so smile! Any promotion can be a great promotion.

Know you are being watched. Suppose there are only a few people in the bookstore the day you have a signing. Suppose you are bored, and you keep checking your emails, playing an online game, yawning and maybe even looking through a magazine. Now, what if just one of the shoppers is a teacher, a school principal, a newspaper reporter or any other person who could possibly influence your career in a positive way? I have actually encountered all these people, and more, at my signings. My books were "discovered" at a book signing by a gift-shop distributor. I'll say no more.

Present yourself in a positive way. Authors do signings to present themselves and their books. So, smile! Be inviting! Remember that body language speaks louder than words. Sitting with your arms crossed tells people that you are unapproachable. Working crossword puzzles or talking on a cell phone tells people that you are not interested in them. Offer a smile and a "hello" to everyone who passes by. And please do not chew gum!

Understand that body language speaks volumes. There are many books on body language, and I often think it might help if exhibiting authors, or anyone who deals with the public, would take the time to read one. Avoid crossing your arms, put down that book and phone, place a smile on your face and open yourself up to people. You will be amazed at the results; no one wants to approach a curmudgeon.

Dress appropriately. As a children's book author, you may choose to dress as a character in your book. This is always a plus and is a great way to attract children. At least a funny hat or some type of prop will do. I wear my fairy wings and antenna, and children can't help but notice me. It's true that you only have one chance to make a good first impression. If you are not dressing as one of your characters, business casual dress is safe, as long as you realize that casual in this case also means tasteful. No sloppy jeans or hooded sweatshirts, please. For the ladies, no tank tops, and go easy with the jewelry and makeup.

Ignore your chair. Yes, stand up. Whoever said authors must sit? I use my chair for my jacket and purse, and nothing more. The best way to look someone in the eye is to be at their eye level. Smile and chat with customers as they walk by, and hand each one a bookmark. My rule of thumb is to only sit when I have more than 50 people waiting in my line.

Set up your table. Bring a nice table cover, preferably one with a theme that fits your book. A fabric store is a good place to find an inexpensive cover. Have business cards, bookmarks, school brochures (see the section titled "School Visits Part One: Create a School Brochure"), a pad of stick-on note paper, a few pens and a bottle of water. I also keep a bottle of anti-bacterial hand cleaner and a small box of tissues in my purse. Rather than start a signing with a table piled high with too many stacked books, I keep about ten books on the table, the rest underneath, and replenish them as necessary. I don't want people to say, "Wow, look at all those books. It doesn't look like she has sold *any*."

Write your own announcement for the intercom. Most large stores are happy to have an employee announce your presence in the store. Sometimes the employee isn't sure what to say, so it's a good idea to write your own short announcement. A few sentences about who you are, the name of your book, and where in the store you are located will suffice. You may also want to (nicely) remind the employee to make the announcement several times, especially if there's a lull in the traffic.

Be careful at group signings. One thing you don't want to do at a group signing is spend your time chatting with the other authors. You are there to reach out to people and promote your book, and customers may feel uncomfortable interrupting your "chat-fest." I always make it my private personal goal to outsell the other authors; that keeps me on task. I am friendly, but I don't have time to chat.

Know where to sign the book. There's no law governing the right or wrong place to sign a book, although the standard place to sign is the title page; it really comes down to your personal preference. Most authors prefer blue or black ink; colored inks are rarely used. You can use a ballpoint or a good quality rollerball or drawing pen. Just be sure you have a few pens with you of a type that will not smear, blot or bleed.

Decide what your autograph will say. I was so excited at my first signing that it never dawned on me to plan what I was going to say. I have since learned that it helps to have about three stock phrases in mind that you can rotate when signing books. This is also helpful when you need to be able to chat with people while thinking about what you are writing.

Always ask people to spell their names. The number of different ways to spell names is nothing short of astounding. I thought I was safe when I signed a book to *Lee*, and embarrassed when I learned that it was spelled *Li*. Since that day, I always ask. I had one customer look at me as if I were loony when she told me the child's name was *Mary* and I asked her how it was spelled. Little did she know I had already signed a book that day to *Maree*. It helps to bring a pad of stick-on notes along to have people write the names for you. On the occasions that I have made a mistake with the signature, I have traded the book for a good copy that I had in my car, put a sticker over the name, and later donated the book. (This is a good reason to always have extra books in your car.)

Where Else Can I Have a Book Signing?

While a local bookstore is an ideal place for a book signing, you can also try thinking outside the box for a different venue. For example, if your book is about a dog, you may want to consider asking at a local pet store if they would be interested in hosting an event. If your book is about a horse, try a tack shop. Toy stores are another good venue for children's books. I have found most store owners to be very cooperative when an event will involve bringing more customers into their stores. I have even had signings in a local beauty salon for my book *The Knot Fairy,* which is all about tangled hair. Be sure you discuss the business end of the event with your host before the event. In most cases, they will prefer to run the sales through their registers and then give you the agreed upon percentage. In my experience, most stores have requested a 40 to 50% discount, which is reasonable. Don't expect to hold an event in someone's place of business and not share the profits.

Impromptu Book Signings. Impromptu book signings are something I never planned for, and had never heard of, hence the name "impromptu book signings." It all began innocently enough when I was having lunch at a popular chain restaurant with a fellow author. She was leaving for a book festival that I was unable to attend, and she offered to take some of my books to sell at her booth. I placed a pile of my books on the table and proceeded to sign them, when lo and behold, restaurant patrons and employees started coming to the table to ask if they could see the books. I sold five books at lunch and handed out lots of bookmarks. The seed was planted. No, I don't take books with me to every restaurant; however, I have, on a few other occasions, taken a few books with me when meeting friends for lunch. I have made sales several more times at different restaurants and even a few times at airports. I'm just saying!

The bottom line: The success of a book signing isn't measured only by the number of books you sell. Of course you want to sell books, but if you have met and interacted with young readers and their parents, made a few contacts, or connected with other authors, it was a day well spent.

If you believe in your books and believe in yourself, you will realize you have accomplished something that many people only dream about. Be proud! Oh, and did I say smile?

31. What Happens in Story Time Stays in Story Time

M any libraries and bookstores have story time hours, some as often as several times a week. As a children's book author, these are good venues for honing your skills as a reader. Of course you can read, but can you read and smile at the same time? Can you read and smile and listen to a crying child at the same time? Can you read and smile and listen to a crying child while having sticky little fingers unbuckle your new shoes? You get the idea. Story times are unpredictable, mainly due to the age of the children who attend, often two to four years old, and with very short attention spans.

Expect the Unexpected

I've been a guest author at lots of story times. Just for fun, I'd like to tell you about some actual story time experiences that I have had. These are all true stories. At one story time, while I was reading my book, a grown man and his toddler son were actually rolling on the floor having a serious wrestling match over a toy truck that the child just wanted to hold while he listened to the story. Then there were the two little girls who spent the entire hour hitting each other over the head with plastic flowers they had brought from home. Add to that the two nannies I spotted sound asleep in the front row while their little charges wandered aimlessly around the room. Oh yes, and there was also an entire preschool class proudly carrying the fairy wands they had just made in honor of my visit. Wands were waving, kids were being poked, and all I could hear was my mother's voice in my head saying, "Stop that before you poke someone's eye out!" And it's funny how there always seems to be at least one "Cheerio Kid" at each story time, because after each event, the floor is always dotted with cereal. Just remember: No matter what happens, smile and have fun!

Valuable for Children and Author

I don't mean to belittle story time at all. I actually love these events and find them extremely valuable to children and authors. For many children, attending story times will make a huge impact on their learning to read. For some, it may be their only exposure to books. As an author, if you plan to also visit schools, story time can be a wonderful way to perfect your skills in reading and smiling at the same time, while holding your book in front of you with the pictures facing the audience. Here's a helpful hint: Memorize your book. That way you can fully enjoy the view from the front of the room, an experience that will add personality and excitement to each event.

Story time is usually not a time to make a lot of book sales. However, it is a place to meet people and spread the word about your book. If you are visiting a local library or bookstore, it is a way to make yourself known in the community. I always take bookmarks or postcards with me and make sure each child leaves with one. This is also a good place to distribute coloring pages depicting characters or scenes from your book. These are relatively easy and inexpensive to produce. If the illustrator will give you some of the final illustration sketches before the color is added, you can simply add the title of the book, along with your website address, and you have coloring pages. Some home printers have a "coloring book" setting that will print any picture as a black and white coloring page.

Visit your local library and schedule a few visits. Then smile and have fun.

32. School Visits
Part One: Create a School Brochure

When children have an opportunity to meet an author, a special connection is often made. The children become energized and motivated as they experience a new appreciation for reading. I know, because I've visited many schools—as a teacher, a parent, and now as an author. I've spent many magical days looking into children's inquisitive eyes.

When you contact school secretaries or media specialists about scheduling a visit, most will request that you send more information. Be prepared with a professional-looking brochure. In many cases, this will be their first look at who you are, so it needs to be clear, concise and easy to read. Check carefully for spelling and grammatical errors and, if possible, see if perhaps your editor could lend an extra pair of eyes.

Brochures are relatively easy to create. The many online printing companies offer templates to guide you. Following the template, you simply add your own information, upload a few photos, and choose your own color scheme. A trifold brochure will give you enough space to add the important information. Be sure to watch for sales, and take advantage of the discounts. Start by ordering a small quantity of brochures—perhaps 25; you may want to change or add information as you perfect your presentation or receive new reviews or awards.

Be sure to include:

- A photo of yourself, preferably reading to a group of children (Remember your focus group? They would love to be in your photo.)

- A short, enticing description of the program you offer

- Your bio as it relates to children

- The grade level of your target audience

- The number of presentations you will do during each visit, along with the number of children you prefer to have in each group

- A short description of your book

- A picture of your book cover

- Reviews of both your book and your presentation (These may have to be added to future printings if you are just embarking on this new adventure.)

- Your contact information

- Your website information

- Your fee if you choose to include it (I prefer to let people know in advance what my fee will be.)

Let's talk about fees. Deciding what to charge for your visit is always a difficult decision. You are likely concerned that if you charge too little, it will appear that you are not worthy; yet if you charge too much, you may not be hired. Remember that, as an author, you have gone through a process that not many people have accomplished. You have something to say that is interesting to both students and teachers. You have spent hours putting together your props and other materials, and you will be spending time traveling to and from these visits. That being said, there is a staggering range of fees that authors charge. I have talked to authors who charge $75 for a visit, and others whose fees are $1,200. Weigh your experience and your location. Factor in the length of your presentation and the fact that you will end up putting in a full day of work, even for a half-day presentation. You can also talk to teachers or other authors in your area for suggestions.

Important: Do not put any photos on the Internet, or any other public forum, that show children's faces unless you have written permission from their parents. Have the photos taken from the back of the room, showing only the children's backs.

Sample School Brochure

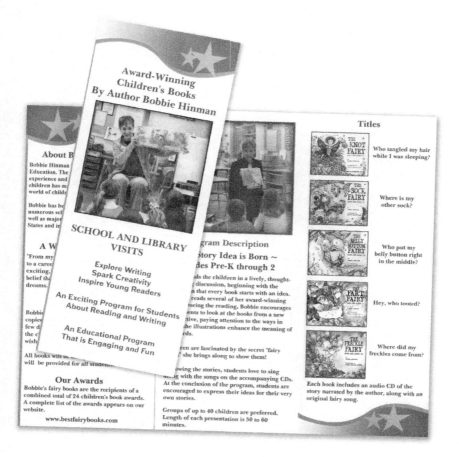

32. School Visits
Part Two: How to Plan a Successful School Visit

As your new career as an author and presenter begins, be prepared to spend a considerable amount of time promoting yourself to the schools in your area. If you do a good job, word will travel fast, and you will likely be invited to visit many other schools. Before you head down this road, there are some things you should know about planning a visit:

Make the initial contact. Compile a list of private and public elementary schools in your area. You may also want to add preschools. Call each one on your list. A few calls a day will be fine if you feel overwhelmed with the process. Introduce yourself and ask for the name and contact information (usually an email address) of the person who handles the author visits at that particular school. It may be the school secretary, the media specialist or a PTA member. Be sure to also get the name of the person to whom you are speaking, so when you make the next phone call, you can say who referred you. When you speak to the correct person, give a very brief introduction of yourself and your books and tell them you will be happy to send further information. Be sure to ask for their mailing address.

Send a cover letter and brochure. The next step is to send a letter confirming your conversation, along with your shiny new brochure. If you have already visited schools and have taken photos, put together a photo collage. Be especially sure to include photos that show you smiling, with eager little children raising their hands. I usually ask teachers to take a few photos at each of my visits. **Remember:** Do not put any photos on the Internet, or any other public forum, that show children's faces unless you have written permission from their parents. Have the photos taken from the back of the room, showing only the children's backs.

Make a follow-up phone call. Wait about a week, and no longer than ten days, before you make the follow-up call. Politely ask if they have had a chance to look at your information. Tell them you are setting up your schedule and will be happy to set up a date. If they hesitate, I always ask if they would like to see a copy of the book. If so, I put a book in the mail, along with another friendly letter. This necessitates yet another follow-up call. Whether or not the final decision is to have me visit the school, I always tell them to keep the book as a donation to their media center.

Discuss the number and size of the groups you prefer. When you get a "yes" for your visit, this is the time to discuss the number of presentations you will do in a day, along with the number of children you prefer to have in each group. My preference is three sessions in one day, each with 40 to 45 children. Some authors are comfortable doing large assembly-type presentations, however I prefer the smaller groups. When children are excited, they have a lot to share, and being in a smaller group allows this to happen. For children in preschool through first grade, I like the proximity of showing an actual book to a small group, rather than showing pictures of the book on a large screen. Second graders and above are more likely to be able to sit longer and pay attention in a larger venue without too much fidgeting.

Email an order form for the teachers to send home with the children. Explain that, once a date has been set, you will be emailing the contact person an order form to be copied and sent home with the children before your visit. Be sure to verify the email address of this contact person. Then, a week before your visit, email the form, requesting that it be sent home with the children within the next two or three days. I always request that they print the order form on colored paper so it will stand out among the other school papers the children normally bring home. The forms are to be completed by the parents and sent back to school, along with payment for the ordered books.

Bring books with you. On the day of the visit, bring enough books to cover a reasonable number of purchases, such as half the number of books as children, plus a few extras for teachers who may also wish to have their own copies. A small wheeled suitcase is ideal for carrying the books. After my presentations, I ask for a quiet corner, either in the media center or an empty classroom, where I can sit and sign the books. The teachers should have the orders and checks that the children have returned to the school. Some authors prefer to take the orders home, sign the books, and bring them back the following day.

Ask the teachers for reviews. As I leave the school, I give the participating teachers a few of my business cards and ask if they would be willing to write a one- or two-sentence review of my presentation and email it to me. These reviews can be added to future brochures.

This may all seem overwhelming, and I'll admit it was at first. But if you work hard in the beginning, before you know it, teachers will be calling *you*.

To be perfectly honest, there are many, many authors who are interested in arranging school visits, putting school personnel in the position of having to pick and choose. The more "credible" you are, the more likely you are to be accepted. What does this mean? If you are a former teacher, if your books have received awards, or if you have testimonials from other teachers, you are likely to be deemed "more credible." If not, don't give up; you may just have to work a little harder. Offer a few free visits, do a great job, give the children bookmarks, and ask the teachers to write one- or two-sentence reviews of your program. You will gain experience and valuable feedback, in addition to testimonials for your brochure.

Sample School Letter to Parents

Dear Parents,

We are pleased to announce that award-winning author Jane Doe has been invited to present her new fairy book to our students. She will be visiting our school on **January 1st**. You will have the opportunity to purchase personally autographed copies of her book for your child. Ms. Doe will be donating $3 to the school for each book purchased by our students. Please use the form below and return order forms to your child's teacher by the day of the event, **January 1st.**

About The Book
The Library Fairy is a mischievous little fairy who visits children while they explore the library shelves, and is responsible for helping them choose just the right book. Each book comes with an audio CD of the story narration and an original fairy song. *The Library Fairy* has recently received the following award:
~ Fairy's Choice Gold Medal ~

About The Author
Jane Doe has a B.S. Degree in Education and, after teaching kindergarten for 25 years, is now pursuing her dream of writing. Her delightful books capture children's imaginations and encourages their love of reading. Please visit www.justafairy.com to learn more about Jane Doe and her books. We are excited to celebrate the success of an award-winning children's book author and former teacher, and communicate the inspiration behind Jane's work to our students.

_____

I would like to purchase_____ copies of *The Library Fairy* at $16.95.

for a total of _____. Autograph to_____.

Please make checks payable to ***Just a Fairy***.

Child's
Name_____Teacher_____

32. School Visits
Part Three: Authors, Please Don't Put Them to Sleep!

Once you've made the decision to conduct classroom visits, you will realize that there's more to it than just reading a book to a happy group of children. Anyone can read a book. A presentation is a different story (no pun intended).

As I look into the adorable little faces of the classroom children, a question always crosses my mind: Am I engaging? I think the answer is "yes." At least I hope so. I'm not talking about "engaging," as in attractive or delightful. I'm talking about the word "engaging" when used as a verb. Most parents and teachers have probably realized that the longer you talk to children, the less they hear. Talk too long and they hear nothing...nada. Engage them and you have an entirely different situation.

Here are a few clues to indicate whether the group you are reading to is showing signs of boredom:

- The children's eyes appear to have glazed over.
- They start pushing or tickling each other.
- You ask a child a question, and the answer is, "Huh?"
- You ask the group a question, and no one raises their hand.
- You tell a joke, and no one even smiles.
- You ask a question about your book, and someone raises a hand to tell you a totally unrelated story about her new cat.

Now don't get me wrong. I'm in no way suggesting that we act like clowns or try to be entertainers. Nevertheless, it's really important to engage the children and ask them questions throughout your presentation. Here are some suggestions to rev up your presentations:

Bring props. Wear a silly hat or something else that ties in to your story. Bring some props to show the class, such as a lantern similar to one that might appear in your book, or a stuffed toy that looks like an animal in your book. I wear fairy wings, which always attracts attention, and I bring along a small treasure chest. I'm very secretive about what lies within the chest, and I bring the items out one by one throughout the story. For example, if I'm reading *The Sock Fairy,* I bring out a pair of my mismatched socks, a situation I blame on the fairy. Then I show the class a very tiny pair of socks that I claim belong to the Sock Fairy. This is a good way to keep their attention because they are always wondering what interesting item I will pull out of my treasure box next.

Can you interject a song? If your book comes with an audio CD that features a recorded song, you can have the children listen to the music and then sing along as you play it again. If you don't have a CD, perhaps you can find a song with a theme that fits your book. You could also make up a song or rhyme to teach them. For children with short attention spans, a change in activities is important. It's a good idea to bring along your own CD player to avoid any scrambling on the part of the teacher to help you set up.

Have the children repeat words aloud. Have the group repeat a word that you have used, or have them read aloud with you a word or line of text. In one of my books, the word "hush" comes at the end of a rhyme, and I always have the class say the word with me, stretching the word as long as they can while saying it as quietly as they can. Another of my stories has the character "shouting with glee," so this is where I give them a chance to shout. Needless to say, this is always big hit.

Bring colorful pictures or charts. These can be illustrations from your book that you have enlarged to show comical details that might otherwise be hard for the children to see. Another idea might be to show a map of where your story takes place. As a rule, children love to look for hidden items in a picture and also love to come up to the front of the class to point to items they can identify. *The Sock Fairy* ends with an elaborate illustration of the fairy's house, loaded with socks of every size and color. After I read the book, I hold up an 18x24-inch mounted enlargement of this illustration and ask if anyone can guess how many socks are in the picture, or if they see any of *their* missing socks in his house. This is another way to keep the class engaged. Perhaps you even have a picture of the cover of your next book that you could talk about.

Give each child a bookmark. Bookmarks are great marketing devices, and children love to receive them. If you sign up for emails with several online printing companies, you will be able to purchase bookmarks when you are notified of a sale. It's easy to create your own designs on these sites. Just be sure your bookmarks include a picture of your cover, along with your name, website and contact information.

Compliment your audience. I learned this in my teaching career: Tell them several times what good listeners they are, and it will become a self-fulfilling prophecy.

Wrap it up with a sharing session. By the time you finish your program, the children will probably be bursting with thoughts they want to share. I like to end the session with a question. In my case it's a question about fairies. Each of the fairies in my books is responsible for one of life's little mysteries, so I ask, "If you were to write a story about a fairy, what would *your* fairy do?" Then I sit back and prepare to be amazed at their very creative answers. Tie your question in to your story, such as "Where do you think Scruffy will go on his next adventure?"

Do what you can to change the pace and keep things moving so you can hold the children's attention. Generally, the entire presentation should not be longer than 45 minutes for preschoolers, and an hour for first graders.

Make the children a part of the experience rather than just a group of onlookers. You've probably heard that expression, "I see your lips moving, but all I hear is blah, blah, blah." Don't let that happen to you.

33. Book Fairs and Other Festivals

Book fairs and festivals are far and away my favorite area of marketing. I love being among book lovers and writers, and meeting my customers face-to-face. I love to see the smiles on children's faces when they look at my books. I love the excitement of setting up my booth and seeing the early shoppers rush into the fair. I love selling my books at retail. I love it all! But be prepared; it's not quite that easy. Let's take a look, from beginning to end, at what's really involved in making it happen.

Search for events. An Internet search is a good way to start looking for fairs. You can Google "book fairs," "book festivals" and "reading festivals" to find events in your area. Depending on where you live, you may want to also Google these events in neighboring states. You can ask other authors for recommendations and watch the events section of your local newspaper. Keep in mind that most book fairs post their applications online four to six months prior to the event, so planning ahead is imperative.

Before you apply. If you have read the online information for an event and you still have questions, call the organizer and obtain the answers you need to make an educated decision about whether this particular event fits your schedule and budget. It's also a good idea to inquire about previous attendance numbers and whether the fair is held indoors or outdoors.

Ask to be a presenter. Once you have chosen a particular event, you can contact the organizer by phone and request to be placed in an area near other children's books, and to be considered as a presenter. A presentation usually involves a reading of your book on a stage or other designated area. This short presentation usually gets your name on the event schedule, which hundreds, or even thousands, of attendees will see. If you are chosen, you will have this accolade to use when contacting other event coordinators, and, if you do a nice job, you will probably be considered for the next year's fair. Being a presenter will mean being away from your booth for about thirty minutes, so it helps to bring a friend or family member along to take care of your booth while you are presenting.

What will it cost? Entry costs vary greatly. Some fairs are one-day events; others involve two or three days. A one-day fair may cost $75 to $150, while a two-day fair may be $400. Again, this varies, so you will have to read the information carefully when you apply. You should probably get your feet wet by starting with a local fair so you don't incur travel and hotel costs on top of the entry fees.

What is included? Most of the time you will be given a designated space, a table and two chairs. Table sizes vary and are almost always mentioned on the registration form. Many times a tent is included (for outdoor fairs); other times you will have to bring your own. Sometimes there is also a small sign provided with your company name. Often there is a printed brochure for attendees that lists the exhibitors along with their booth numbers. Occasionally there are volunteers around to help you carry your items to your booth; usually you will have to do it yourself.

Should you discount your books? That's entirely up to you. Most customers like a discount. Don't you? If you prefer, instead of a discount, you can try a giveaway. See the section titled "Gifts, Gimmicks and Giveaways" for pricing and giveaway ideas. Whatever price you determine should be clearly printed on a small sign at your table.

Gather your supplies. In addition to your display materials (see below), be sure to pack bookmarks, school brochures, tape, scissors, pens, lots of change, and something to hold your money. Some people use a money box, but I feel safer with a zipper pouch that I can wear around my waist. You may also need a hand truck for carrying your supplies to your booth. I have found it easy to carry the small supplies in a plastic tub, which I have nicknamed my "didja box." After asking my husband so many times, "didja remember to bring" this or "didja remember to bring" that, it seemed like an appropriate name.

Design Your Booth Display

The goal is to showcase your book and draw people into your booth. No run-of-the-mill bed sheet for a table cover allowed!

Visit a fabric store. Choose an attractive cloth in colors that will enhance your book, but not a busy pattern that will compete. Think bright! Think cheerful! Think inviting! I always use sparkly fabrics. Believe it or not, I have even had people at fairs ask to buy my table covers. Tables at book fairs usually range in size from six to eight feet long, so plan for the longest size and add three feet on each end, making a fourteen-foot length of fabric. If the table is shorter, you can always fold the fabric under. Also, choose the widest width fabric available (usually fifty-four inches) because most festivals will want your cloth to reach the floor on the customers' side.

"Present" your book! You *could* do something ordinary like put your book in a book rack or, if you have multiple titles, set up a bookshelf, or something really boring like place your books in a stack on the table. Or you could think outside the box. I like this idea better. *Present* your book! One of my tricks is to create height by using varying sizes of small boxes that I place on the table and then cover with fabric or brightly colored scarves. I place a book on top of each box, using an attractive book rack.

{ 197 }

For another effect, I have used glass blocks that I purchased at a hardware store, each draped with a scarf and topped with a book in a decorative rack. My most recent display includes inexpensive square plastic food storage containers (lighter in weight than glass blocks), each draped with a scarf and topped with a book. Going one step further, I have now added LED string lights inside the plastic boxes to highlight each book with glowing lights. By the way, the scarves and lights I use are all purchased at a dollar store and are usually available in many themes and colors. Another hint: Even if you have just one book, display multiple copies so the table won't look bare.

Plan a backdrop. The back of the booth is also important. Many times a booth will back up to another booth or a plain wall, or even worse—an ugly wall. Sometimes there is a curtain already in place, sometimes not. For outdoor events, where a tent is usually necessary, you can order an enlargement of your book cover on a banner made of a canvas-type material, with grommets at the top for hanging. (It's time to revisit your favorite online printing company.) A pretty rope from the fabric store can be used to hang the banner across the back of your booth. Multiple books means multiple banners on the rope, creating a nice effect. Occasionally I have been in situations where there is no way to attach the rope; so, for these events, I use a large, collapsible stand-up sign, also purchased online.

For indoor events, where wind is not an issue, I use two folding screens that I purchased at a discount furniture store. Across the top of the screens, I drape glittery scarves or strings of multi-colored, battery-operated LED lights. I created a sign with my company name by using wooden letters from an art-supply store, and hang it with ribbon in the center of the folding screens. The effect is dramatic and eye-catching. The secret here is to be creative, and think inexpensive and easy-to-assemble.

Anything Else?

Yes, I have a few more important bits of advice:

Use a credit card reader. I highly recommend this. Many people rely on their credit cards, and you don't want to ever have to turn a customer away. There are a number of easy-to-use card readers available, and all you need is a cell phone or tablet to use them. It's important to note that occasionally there is no Wi-Fi available, and you will have to rely on a cellular connection.

Arrive early. There are always early-birds, eager to shop. I open my boxes and pull some books out quickly, even before the rest of the booth is set up, so I am always ready to show a book to an early shopper.

Don't put all your books on the table. Your display copies plus a few of each title are enough to put on the table. Keep the rest under the table where you can reach them quickly, as you need them. Don't pile them up on the table. You don't want a large pile of books to give the impression that you haven't sold any.

Make a "Meet The Author" sign. A simple, small sign on your table or taped to the wall will do. It's surprising how many people don't realize that *you* are the author. An author friend of mine even had a T-shirt printed with "Yes, I AM the author!" across the front.

Pricing sign. This can be a small sign, propped in a book rack on your table. You should also mention on the sign that you take credit cards.

Give bookmarks away freely. Make sure your book cover image, contact information and website appear on your bookmarks. Often, people will order at a later date. Don't let anyone slip away empty-handed.

Try not to sit down. Stand and engage people. It may help to purchase a rubberized mat to stand on. Look like you are having fun. Talk, smile, hand out bookmarks. Look approachable!

Don't eat at the booth. An important reason to bring a friend, in addition to the help and moral support he or she provides, is to have someone take over for you when you are hungry or need a bathroom break. There are few scenarios worse than taking a big bite of food and having a customer come up to your booth and ask you a question. You get the picture. If bringing a helper isn't possible, I'm not suggesting you go hungry. Just be discreet.

Use clear plastic bags. This way, your customers can advertise for you and help drive people to your booth as they stroll around the fair. For purchasing bags, I look for the best online deals, even if it means ordering a large quantity. I never have to rely on the dreaded grocery bags.

Smile all day! Even if you are standing on cement and your feet and back hurt. Even if you haven't sold as many books as you would like.

Other Festivals

In addition to book fairs, there are many other venues available to authors for showcasing and selling children's books. Sometimes the theme or location of your story will give you an idea that will help you begin your search.

Festivals with a theme. Since my books are about fairies, I have found Fairy Festivals to be a productive sales arena. There are other festivals, such as Renaissance Fairs, Pirate Fairs, DragonCon and ComicCon that may fit the theme of your book.

Holiday fairs. Check the local newspapers and online for any schools or churches in your area that are having holiday fairs or bazaars. I have found these to be very lucrative. There are normally very few book vendors at these bazaars, and books make great gifts. Organizations such as the YMCA, Boy Scouts and Girl Scouts often have holiday or seasonal fairs. This is an ideal way to showcase your book to families in your area, and make contacts for school presentations.

Street fairs. Who doesn't love a street fair? Most small towns have these fun fairs for various holidays such as Christmas and the 4th of July. You are also likely to find fairs such as country fairs, farm fairs, harvest celebrations and art festivals. Most of these events feature a variety of vendors, and many are relatively inexpensive to enter.

Farmers markets. Also called Green Markets, these events are springing up all over. They are inexpensive to enter and are attended by lots of families. Why not give one a try?

Monthly events. Many towns have monthly celebrations. From First Sundays to First Fridays, these block-party-type events often feature music, food and vendors.

Children's events. Scour your local newspaper for these events. There are children's Christmas and Hanukah Fairs, Easter Fairs, Baby and Toddler Fairs, etc. Be creative in your searching. You may be surprised at the number of places where you and your books will fit in.

Think about this: Many fairs and festivals target shoppers who are looking for gifts, rather than purchasing for themselves. Have you thought of your book as a gift item? If it has broad appeal, a timely subject and an outstanding cover, it will fit nicely into the gift-giving arena.

Examples of Booth Displays

34. Should You Ever Give Your Books Away?

I have asked many fellow authors whether or not they believe in giving away sample copies of their books. The results seem to fall equally on both sides of the fence. The main reason cited for not giving away books is that, "if someone is genuinely interested, they should at least be willing to cover the cost of the book." Also heard a few times was the argument that "my books are not free to me, so why should they be free to others?"

On the other side of the fence, my freebies have resulted in some very large sales. I recently visited a major bookstore that did not have my books on the shelf. I asked the manager if she would be interested in ordering a few books and added that I would be happy to come back to sign them when they came in. Since she was not familiar with my books, I handed her a copy of each, along with my contact information and some bookmarks, and told her they were a gift to help her become acquainted with the books. I also suggested that she use them as display copies to generate interest. A week later I received a call from the manager saying that she did display the books and had also read them during story time. In addition, she had held a drawing in the store on a busy Saturday, using one of the books as a prize. She thanked me for sharing the books with her and asked me to please stop by in a few days to sign the 30 books that she had ordered for her store. She requested a book signing, which we scheduled that day. Just think, all this from three sample books!

That same day, I dropped off copies of my books to an upscale children's boutique. I introduced myself to the owner and gave her the books, again as a gift, which I assured her would enhance the already wonderful gift selection in her store. This time I only had to wait two days before she called to place an order.

One more example: While exhibiting at a book fair, I was approached by a man who asked if I would like to sell my books in Costco. I kicked my poor husband, who was standing next to me, in the shins, tried to keep a straight face, and then answered that, of course, I wouldn't mind. He asked for samples. By that time I had four titles. Yes, I gave him four books, not knowing if he was the real deal. He was, and I have done many book signings at Costco stores ever since.

If a school requests a copy of a book after receiving my school brochure, that book becomes a gift whether or not they choose to have me do a presentation. I also give free books to my close friends and relatives, who have turned out to be quite vocal when it comes to sharing my books with *their* friends and relatives, resulting in many, many sales.

A Few Guidelines That I Use:

Be free, but not too free, with your freebies. This is where some common sense and gut feelings come into play. I don't want to give the impression that I recommend standing on the corner handing out free books. In the cases I've cited above, my gut feeling was to give the books away; in most cases, I give away books only if the person seems genuinely interested and if I feel there is a very good chance of it leading to a sizable sale.

Don't take the books back. If a store manager decides not to purchase the books, I don't go back to reclaim them. I tell the manager the books were a gift. You never know what will come of it.

Be sure to exchange contact information. If you give a book to a prospective customer, be sure you leave your contact information. This means a professional business card, a colorful postcard, or a brochure, not a scribbled cell number on a scrap of paper. Also, be certain you have *their* contact information.

Be sure to follow up. While people mean well, many need a friendly reminder. I follow up on every free book, in person if at all possible. When face to face, you are more likely to make the sale.

Books for charities. I believe in giving back whenever possible. I am happy that my autographed books are welcomed as raffle items at charity events. The publicity generated by being featured in their marketing materials is also an added benefit.

Don't forget: Be sure to ask your tax professional if you are entitled to a tax deduction for the books you give away as promotional items.

35. Cards for Kids

As an author of children's books, you should always be your own best advocate. Be on the lookout for eye-catching promotions you can use. But don't overlook business cards, a traditional tool that continues to be very effective for promoting business. Business cards are attention getters; they let people know who you are and what you have to offer. Giving out business cards is crucial to marketing your skills or services. But what if many of your clients are children? Why not have a *special* card to give to them?

I have found that colorful postcards work as well for children as traditional business cards do for adults. I hand them out to children I meet at schools, libraries, restaurants, book fairs, the grocery store and the airport. Yes, there are always lots of restless children in every airport. I carry the cards wherever I go. I have always been the type to strike up a conversation with people I meet in the grocery line or at nearby tables in restaurants; now I introduce myself to the parents and make sure each child I meet goes home clutching a colorful fairy postcard. Many parents have thanked me for providing this diversion for fussy children. As I mentioned earlier, there are a number of online companies that offer great prices on custom cards. Watch for sales and stock up.

You can do a lot of marketing for your money if you use the cards wisely and abundantly.

Here are some design and marketing tips for my "Cards for Kids" program:

- Make the cards colorful and attractive, and be sure to feature a picture of your book cover.

- Include your name, website and ISBN, plus any pertinent ordering information.

- Add a *very short*, yet enticing, blurb about your book.

- Turn the back of the card into a miniature coloring page by adding a black and white picture of one of your characters.

- Be generous. Hand out lots of cards.

- Never leave home without them. Always have extras in your car.

- Maximize every "perchance" meeting.

- Use them as bookmarks in the books you are reading so you'll always have them readily available if you meet someone at school, at a book club, in the gym or wherever you go where you might carry a book.

- Have your spouse, family and friends carry your cards to give to people they meet.

Short of renting a helicopter and dropping cards from the sky, this is one of the best ways I have found to spread the word.

Samples of Cards for Kids

Front

Coming soon...

THE BELLY BUTTON FAIRY
BOOK AND AUDIO CD
BY
BOBBIE HINMAN
ILLUSTRATED BY
MARK WAYNE ADAMS

Back

Best Fairy Books
1-800-782-4115
www.Bestfairybooks.com

Dear _____

I love The Knot Fairy!
I love The Sock Fairy!

Guess what's coming next -
The Belly Button Fairy!
I can hardly wait!

Your friend,
_____

Be sure to watch my website
for updates.
Bobbie Hinman, Author

The Knot Fairy - ISBN 978-0-9786791-0-1
The Sock Fairy - ISBN 978-0-9786791-1-8
The Belly Button Fairy - ISBN 978-0-9786791-3-2

Back

COLOR ME! THE KNOT FAIRY

Front

Best Fairy Books
Award-Winning Children's Picture Books
with Audio CDs
www.bestfairybooks.com

THE KNOT FAIRY
THE SOCK FAIRY
THE BELLY BUTTON FAIRY
THE FART FAIRY

By Bobbie Hinman

36. Gifts, Gimmicks and Giveaways

When selling your book through your website, or at venues such as book fairs and other festivals, you have the unique opportunity to give things away. I *like* to give things away. Why? Because *I* like it when someone gives *me* a gift. I also like the fact that it makes my young customers happy. I've tried a lot of giveaways throughout my career as an author. I'd like to share with you my successes and my not-too-successful attempts. It's important to keep in mind that anything you give away needs to be child-friendly, meaning it can have no sharp points and must be too large to swallow. It's not easy to find a giveaway that is safe and cheap enough to purchase in bulk, yet has perceived value to the customer. But if parents are at the tipping point when deciding whether or not to purchase a book, a gift often helps them decide in your favor, especially when the child wants the gift.

Can You Afford to Give Things Away?

This is an area where your printing costs and the size of your print run come into play. The higher your costs, the less wiggle room you will have. The larger your print run, the lower your costs will be. Print on Demand (POD) customers almost always have costs that allow little room for gifts. If your budget allows just one promotional item, make it an outstanding bookmark. Whatever you choose, be sure it ties into the theme of your book.

Some of My Successful Free-With-Purchase Gifts:

Fairy animals. Purchased from an online wholesale gift site, these plush little animals with wings were my first giveaways. They cost less than $1 each and the customers were thrilled. Even selling the books at a discount, I still made a profit.

Whoopee cushions. I purchase these in bulk from the same online wholesale gift site for 25¢ each, and they are the perfect giveaway with each purchase of *The Fart Fairy*. I have been giving them away for four years and the kids (and many parents) love them!

Bendable figures. These Gumby-like bendable figures, also purchased online, cost about 50¢ each, making them ideal giveaways. I order fairies and sock monkeys, and the kids love them. I have been using them as gifts for several years and they are inexpensive enough that I often give each child more than one.

Plastic drinking cups. These have been one of my most successful gifts. For each of my book launch parties, I have ordered 12-ounce plastic drinking cups imprinted with a drawing of the main character, along with the book title and my website. The cost is about 35¢ each. For a launch party, I fill each cup with items such as a tiny note pad, a few wrapped candies, some removable tattoos and a plastic fairy doll. After the launch parties, I use the cups as book fair giveaways. Kids love them, and moms are happy to receive something useful.

My Not-So-Successful Attempts

Plastic combs. When *The Knot Fairy* was my only book, I thought this was an ideal giveaway. I was so wrong. Kids want toys, not combs. I also found that many young children were used to brushes and weren't even sure what to do with a comb!

Coupons. I tried coupons at one book fair. I gave each customer a coupon for a 25% discount off their next purchase, either in person or online. This was a complete failure. Customers stuffed them into their bags and probably threw everything in the trash. Not one was ever redeemed!

T-shirts. I tried this as an additional sale item, not as a giveaway. It didn't work too well. Actually, to be perfectly honest, it was a complete flop. I had T-shirts made with the cover of my first book on the front. The shirts were very cute. I ordered a variety of children's sizes, but very few people were interested. I decided to donate the shirts and move on.

My Promotional Freebies: No Purchase Necessary

Bookmarks. Always successful, bookmarks are a necessary tool of the trade. I hand them out at book signings, book fairs and library visits. I place one in every book I sell, either in person or through my website. I purchase them in large quantities, usually 1,000 at a time, my goal being to get each one into the hands of a prospective customer. I have found that the larger and more colorful the bookmarks, the more people want them. Online printing companies offer a variety of sizes; my preference is the 2x8-inch size, which is large enough for a picture of your book cover to be easily seen. As with the cover of your actual book, the illustrations on the bookmark should be the main focus. A picture of your book cover says more to a customer than any descriptions you can offer. If you have only one book, you may also be able to fit an additional illustration of your main character, preferably doing something silly. Add the book title, the ISBN, your website and your name.

Kids love stickers. When *The Belly Button Fairy* was released, I had stickers made (also online) that were round and looked like big red buttons. In the center was printed "My Button From The Belly Button Fairy." These were a very big hit at book fairs. I gave them out freely, and it was fun to see how many little ones were walking around the fair with my stickers on their tummies. Having learned from the belly button stickers, I have purchased and given away many types of stickers. I give them to every child who walks by; this always helps drive customers to the booth.

Coloring pages. These are easy to make and inexpensive to produce. You need a clean black-and-white illustration of either the main character or a scene from your book. Your illustrator or graphic designer can help you with this, or you can trace a picture from your book and outline it in black. You may be able to use a copy of one of your early sketches. Coloring pages work best when distributed at indoor events. If you offer them outdoors, they are liable to end up flying all over the place.

Postcards. The many online printing companies are good sources for postcards. Design them like a giant bookmark and hand them out freely. They are very effective. (Be sure to read the section titled "Cards For Kids" for more information.)

Other Discounts

I also offer discounts for multiple purchases at book fairs and festivals. For example, my books retail for $16.95 each, and I may offer a discount of two books for $30, three for $42, and four for $52. Another discount strategy is to offer one book for $15 and each additional book for $14. Yet another is, "Buy Three Books, Get One Free." It's entirely up to you. These are just examples; you can experiment to see which ideas appeal to you, and which will fit your budget.

If a teacher, or a retailer not serviced by my distributor, wants to purchase multiple copies, I generally give them a 45% discount. An example of this type of customer would be the beauty shop owner who purchases *The Knot Fairy* to sell in her salon.

Just remember: Everyone loves a bargain; if you are more likely to purchase an item at a discount, your customers will feel the same way. In my experience, it's better to discount the price or add giveaways, thereby making more sales, than to stick to a rigid price and sell fewer books.

I hope some of these ideas will spark your creativity. Finding items that are inexpensive, desirable, and also safe, is the challenge. The hunt is on...

Everyone loves a giveaway!

Samples of Giveaways

Bendable Figures

Whoopee Cushion

Stickers

Best Fairy Books

Bookmark   Plastic Cups

37. How Important Are Book Awards?

Winning an award is an honor. No matter what field you are in, being an award winner will bring you respect. Award contests are where "the cream rises to the top." If you want your book to be up there, I'll repeat what I have said before: *First you must produce a top-quality book!*

What are the benefits of winning awards? The simple answer is that people are more likely to pick up a book that has an award sticker, which then often translates into more sales. Let's face it, awards add credibility. The recognition and instant respect your book will receive when it "wears" an award medal are as worthwhile as any expensive advertising. You can now and forevermore call yourself an "award-winning" author; your book is now an "award-winning" book. It's as simple as that!

What does it cost to enter an award contest? The costs normally range from as low as $45 to as high as $300. Keep in mind that the entry fee is often per book, per category, so if you enter multiple categories you will be paying much more. It may not be worth blowing your advertising budget by entering the most expensive award contests. My recommendation is only to enter as many *worthwhile* award contests as your budget allows. Each contest will require your sending them several nonreturnable copies of your book; the number of books varies according to the specifications of each sponsor.

Does it matter which contests you enter? There are some awards whose entry forms state that self-published books are not eligible. That's fine because there are other very reputable awards just for you! Winning an award shows the world that your book has been selected by experienced judges from hundreds of competing titles, but the keyword here is "experienced." Use discretion when entering award contests. It is a waste of money competing for obscure awards whose stickers may even cause a few raised eyebrows and doubting smiles. Do some research before you enter. Find out how long the award has been in existence and how the judges are chosen. It's always safe to go with respected awards that have been in existence the longest.

Reputable awards to consider. Lists of the book awards open to self-published books are available online. Some reputable awards, and ones that my books have won, are the Benjamin Franklin Award, Mom's Choice Award, IPPY Award, National Indie Excellence Book Award, Foreword Book-of-the-Year Award, USA Book News Best Books Award and Moonbeam Children's Book Award. This is by no means a comprehensive list, as more awards become available each year. Just do your homework.

Before you enter. The details of the contests vary, so be sure to check each one for submission guidelines, entry fees, deadlines and award dates. Of utmost importance, make sure your book is as perfect as it can be and is worthy of an award. Make sure it has been edited and proofread and approved by your all-important focus group.

Be wary of "Top Book Lists." You may also come across a "deal" asking you to submit your book for a chance to appear on a list of "top books." The chance to win this honor almost always has a hefty fee attached. In most cases, the organizers are not experienced judges, and having your name on this list will get you nowhere, so think twice before you decide where to spend your advertising dollars.

Show Off Your Awards by Posting a Colorful Announcement on Your Social Media Sites

WE WON!!!

BEST FAIRY BOOKS IS PROUD TO ANNOUNCE...

THE KNOT FAIRY

**HAS JUST RECEIVED THE PRESTIGIOUS
BENJAMIN FRANKLIN AWARD
IN THE CATEGORY OF
BEST CHILDREN'S PICTURE BOOKS**

WWW.BESTFAIRYBOOKS.COM

38. How to Have Your Book Reviewed

Should you have your book reviewed? The decision is similar to whether you should enter book award contests. There is one big difference, however: If you don't win an award, you move on; but if you receive a bad review, it could plague you forever. It's important to realize that not all reviews are good. But, good or bad, once posted on the Internet, information never goes away. If you are not so sure about the quality of your book, or haven't had it professionally edited, you may want to forego seeking reviews. Also, it's worth noting that you will need to send a free copy of your book to each reviewer.

Reasons to Seek Reviews

Many people read reviews before they purchase a book. A good review can boost book sales by helping prospective customers make the decision to purchase your book.

Reviews add credibility. A review from a *respected* reviewer can definitely help direct people to your book. Note: The key word here is "respected."

Reviews enhance your advertising possibilities. You can add the reviews to your print and Internet promotions, such as your brochures and website, as well as the back of your book when you reprint.

Reviews offer a way to have your book critiqued. Most reviewers will send you a letter or form pointing out the strengths and weaknesses of your book. Be aware that this is not always a good reason to seek reviews. If you are confident of the quality of your book, this can be a plus; however, if you know your book is weak, you really don't want to have a review posted on the Internet. Instead, work on fixing the problem.

Reviews can help you get your foot in the door. You can use a good review to catch the attention of teachers, librarians, booksellers and readers.

Reasons Not to Seek Reviews

Many people read reviews before they purchase a book. A poor or mediocre review can definitely cause prospective customers to turn away.

There is often a fee charged for a review. More and more reviewers today are charging high prices for their services. This can be up to $500! That money might be better used for other marketing projects.

A bad review won't go away. As I've mentioned, once posted on the Internet, a review is here to stay. It's also worth mentioning that, to their credit, many reputable reviewers will send you a critique and refrain from posting negative reviews online. **Note:** The key word here is "reputable."

A good review is not a magic bullet. Although a good review is definitely a plus, it is not a magic bullet automatically leading to thousands of book sales. Marketing is still the key, and incorporating a positive review is a definite advantage.

Unknown reviewers may not be a help. Unless you have an abundance of reviews, a single review from an unknown reviewer may be worth no more than the piece of paper it is written on. Just be careful when choosing a reviewer.

How to Have Your Book Reviewed

Review sites are constantly changing, so before you send your books off willy-nilly to everyone who offers his or her services, do your research! Some good choices are:

Previously used reviewers. If you have published other books that were reviewed, and you were happy with the results, go back to those reviewers.

Reviewers of self-published books. Seek legitimate sites and publications that review self-published books. Not all are willing to accept them.

Reviewers of children's books. Choose sites and publications that specialize in reviewing children's books.

Bloggers. There are many blogs devoted to children's book reviews, and I have yet to come across any that charge for their reviews. Often bloggers will sponsor a giveaway with a copy of your book as the prize. This win-win situation brings traffic to their blogs while promoting your book. (See more about how this works in the section titled "Social Media Strategy.")

Magazines and related publications. You can send a press release or short letter offering a book for review to reviewers and feature writers of publications related to children, parenting or children's books. Do not send a book along with the release; rather, offer to send them a book at their request.

Customers. Aside from professional reviewers, satisfied customers are often a good source of reviews. While these people may be unknown, having a lot of these reviews will still be a positive statement about your book. With each book sold through my website, I include a letter thanking the customer for purchasing my book and politely asking for a review to be posted either on Amazon, Goodreads or my Facebook page.

Is There a Charge?

As I mentioned before, some reviewers charge a fee. *Kirkus Reviews* and other respected publishing magazines now have programs for reviewing self-published books, currently charging between $300 and $500 for a review. *Publishers Weekly* also has a review program for self-published books, costing about half that price. You will also find other popular reviewers who charge about $50, such as *Midwest Book Review*. You might choose to approach some of the smaller, more independent reviewers. Even factoring in the charges, reviews can be an effective and relatively inexpensive publicity/promotion instrument. There are many online lists. Research, research, research!

A Few Things to Avoid

In addition to being wary of reviewers with high fees, my recommendation is to also be wary of:

Review exchanges. When you promote your book on social media sites, you will no doubt receive messages from other authors wanting to swap reviews. Unless you are familiar with their work, this could become an uncomfortable situation. What if they post a poorly written review about your book? What if they don't like your book and post the review all over the Internet? If you don't like their book, would you feel obligated to write a good review? How would you review a book if the author were of a different nationality and the topic of the book was completely foreign to you? I have experienced all of these situations and hope these real-life scenarios will help guide you in making wise choices.

Reviews from your family members. If you have done your homework and produced a quality book, you don't have to go this route to pad your reviews. Besides, it won't impress anyone, and it may make your relatives feel uncomfortable.

Expensive reviews from unscrupulous pseudo-reviewers. Beware of people who think they are qualified to write a review just because they have written a book or self-published a book or have been a teacher, etc. Some charge up to $500 for their meaningless reviews.

Reviews from your 5th-grade teacher. Of course you were the brightest child in the class; however, your teacher's review, if she mentions how she knows you, will just make people laugh. Yes, I *have* seen this.

Sending books without checking first. This is poor etiquette and can end up being very costly.

It's impossible to list the "good" and "bad" reviewers because it is an ever-changing, ever-growing list. Do your research, look into the many review options that are possible, check the reviewers' credentials, and you will be able to come up with ways to receive reviews and achieve your marketing goals without breaking the bank.

39. A Video Trailer? Yes!

Just as movie trailers advertise movies, a video trailer can help you advertise and spread the word about your book. Video production companies are springing up on the Internet, along with an abundance of wonderful book trailers. Having a video trailer prominently displayed on your website, and of course on YouTube and your other social media sites, is well worth the time it takes to develop an entertaining piece. I must admit I'm still "old school," because I paid someone to create my trailers, but if you are computer savvy, you can take advantage of the many programs online that will help you to do a professional job yourself. I've seen a number of homemade videos, and they can be quite dazzling. I can't think of any downside to having a lively, entertaining trailer to showcase your book. In fact, I can give you a few good reasons why it can help you.

A Video Trailer Can:

- **Target** both the visual and audio senses of your potential reader.

- **Create** an emotional tie to your book.

- **Give** potential readers a preview of the book that will leave them wanting more.

- **Drive** traffic to your website.

- **Place** your book in the limelight.

If You Plan to Produce a Video Trailer:

Watch as many book trailers as you can. By doing so, you can decide what you find attractive and inviting, and put the ideas to use in your trailer.

Make it brief. An ideal length for an effective trailer is about 90 seconds. The good news is that this will force you to consolidate your ideas and communicate just the book's important message.

Make it light and happy. Add a catchy tune if you can. Remember, children and their parents are your target audience. If you have produced an audio format with your book, use that same melody for your background music. The goal is to stir the emotions of your audience and make them want to purchase your book.

Be sure it closely represents your book. Have you ever watched a TV commercial and then asked yourself what the scene you just watched had to do with the product they were selling? Right, lesson learned.

Use illustrations from your book. This is the time to show off the charm and irresistibility of your characters and illustrations. You want the children and parents who watch the trailer to say, "I want that book!"

Don't use captions. Trailers move too fast for children to be able to follow along with words. The pictures and narration will convey your message.

Avoid making it look like hard-sell marketing. Get your message across while making it fun and entertaining. Avoid anything that comes across as "in-your-face" marketing.

End with the image of your title, book cover and website. This is very important. Parents want to see exactly what the book looks like and where to buy it. The end of the video should include both words and pictures, with a brief statement telling exactly where the book can be purchased.

Once you have it, use it. Showcase your trailer on your website. Share it on social media with the goal of directing customers to your website. Once they watch it, you have a greater chance of making a sale. If customers see it on your website, they can rush right to the "Buy" button.

Many large publishing houses are producing video trailers to promote their new releases. Yours can be right out there with the best of them.

40. Writers Associations

Many successful authors will probably agree that it's a good idea for writers and self-publishers to join a few associations. These organizations offer wonderful resources in the form of courses, workshops, publications, and other information that will keep you up to date on publishing trends. Writers associations frequently organize conferences where you can exhibit your book while you mix and mingle with other authors in a networking, face-to-face setting. My favorite part of belonging to associations is the camaraderie.

There are a lot of associations from which to choose, with new ones springing up all around the country. You will find national groups, state groups, groups for children's writers, and so on. It would be a daunting task for me to try to make a list of all the available organizations, so get ready to do some research.

How do you find the right groups to join? The Internet is a good place to start. Every group has a website that you can peruse to see if what they have to offer interests you. For local groups, you can start by asking the librarians in your area; they often have information about what events the local writers are planning. Also, bookstore managers may be able to guide you since many bookstores host groups of writers who gather for critique, feedback, and support.

You may want to start your own small group. Really! Your neighbors may be writing, and you don't even know it.

Recently, at a community party, I mentioned that I was working on a new book. Three people chimed in, saying they were each also working on a book. Another had already written a book, and yet another said she had always wanted to write one. So, we are in the process of starting our own small group. Our goal is to offer advice, opinions and support for each other.

The costs vary. Some writers associations are free; others charge membership fees. Checking the fees will be part of your research.

Don't join them all. Joining too many would be costly, and you would likely find yourself being spread too thin. You may want to choose one national association, one at the state level, and one local. It's entirely up to you.

What is IBPA? The Independent Book Publishers Association, with over 3,000 members, is the largest publishing trade association in the United States. While some large associations are not eager to have independent publishers as members, that's what IBPA is all about. Their vision is "A world where every independent publisher has the tools and knowledge needed to professionally engage in all aspects of the publishing industry." I have been a member for a number of years and have had several articles published in their newsletter. Their monthly publication and website cover many topics for self-publishers, such as legal issues, marketing ideas, industry events, business tips, and so much more. Two other advantages to belonging to the IBPA are: They sponsor the very popular annual Benjamin Franklin Book Awards, and they offer many discounted marketing opportunities. **Note: IBPA is just one example of the numerous writers associations available; this information is offered for educational purposes only and is not meant as an endorsement.**

41. Social Media Strategy

Social Media offers a huge arena for mounting a marketing campaign. When added to the book signings and other face-to-face events, it gives you yet another useful tool in your arsenal of marketing ventures. In my experience, combining both online and in-person approaches leads to excellent results. I have found that after I appear at a large book fair, my website activity increases dramatically. And when I do a lot of online promotions for an upcoming event, more people show up at my book signings. The ideal marketing campaign utilizes both methods working hand in hand.

DO use social media *along with* in-person events; DON'T use it *in place* of face-to-face contact with your customers.

It's All About Connections

All social media sites have one thing in common: They provide a network of people with a place to make connections. It seems that everyone today is online using at least one, and often more, of the available social media platforms. There are so many choices, and it sometimes seems as if more are added every day. In no way do I ever pretend to know about or understand all of them. Many of them came into being long after I started my business. I've latched onto several and experimented with a few others. The important thing is for *you* to choose the ones *you* feel comfortable with. In case you are not already social media-savvy, I will give you a very brief rundown of some of the most popular forums available today.

Blogs. Blogging is one of the oldest forms of social media, having become popular long before we started posting, liking, poking and tweeting. Blogs provide an excellent platform for sharing your knowledge, ideas and accomplishments. A blog can be one of your most effective marketing tools. To get started, choose an overall subject for your blog. Choose a topic related to writing that you know quite a lot about so you will be able to discuss it in depth. Examples of topics might be: reading readiness for toddlers, steps in writing a story, or even how to create a children's picture book. Think about the hurdles you've experienced in relation to the topic and write about how you—and your readers—can work on solving them. From there, you can branch out and add other related topics of interest. When I first starting blogging, I added a site meter to my blog so I could see where my followers were located. I was totally amazed that I was reaching people from all over the world.

You can also use other people's blogs to promote your book. Look for Mommy Blogs and blogs that post reviews about children's books and products. You can contact them by email and offer to give them a copy of your book in return for a review. If they are interested, you will need to send each blogger a book. Be sure to also include information about your website, other books you have written, etc. Often they will ask you if you would like to also take part in a giveaway where they ask their readers to enter a drawing for a free book—one that you will provide. The blog owners will handle the details of the giveaways. You will be contacted with the name of the winner, and your next step is to sign and mail the book. If you choose blogs that have a lot of followers, news of your book will reach a lot of prospective customers.

Facebook. One of the most popular social media platforms, with literally millions of active users, Facebook allows you to create a profile of yourself, upload photos and videos, and share information about yourself and your book. In addition to posting information on your own page, Facebook offers the ability to join "groups" of like-minded people with whom you can also share information about your book. There are groups that fit almost any category you can think of, such as Children's Books, Children's Authors and Illustrators, Kindergarten Teachers, and so on.

Facebook also offers an advertising program that allows you to create ads that will be shown on other users' pages. You can choose your budget, and even specify your target audience based on age range, interests and demographics. The information on how to get started is available on Facebook, and is relatively easy to follow. In experimenting with this ad program, I found that the ads that created the best sell-through rates were the ones where I offered a deep discount or special promotion. When I simply posted an ad with my book covers and blurbs about the books, the response was poor. When I advertised " Buy two books and get one free!" the orders literally started coming to my website within minutes. Make it your goal to drive customers to your website to purchase a book. Your ads need to create excitement, not simply inform.

Twitter. Also extremely popular, Twitter allows members to post short messages called "tweets" that are up to 140 characters in length. People can tweet about what is going on in their lives, along with links to things they think are interesting or useful to their followers. Authors can use Twitter to post about their books, their writing, and their interests, and also follow their customers' tweets. If you are having a book promotion, or have just released the e-book version of your book, you can quickly tweet the information to your readers. Tweeting about what you had for breakfast will turn people away. Nothing to tweet about? Schedule a book event, plan a school or library visit or win an award—then you will have something to tweet about.

Google+. Similar in some ways to Facebook, Google+ offers you the ability to join communities, post info about you and your book, and interact with a community of other people who are also interested in books. There is a large Google+ book community, and authors can share information about their current projects or books they have already published.

LinkedIn. With a slightly different slant, LinkedIn is designed more for the business community. It differs from venues such as Facebook and Twitter in that, unlike other social networks, instead of the goal being to become a friend to everyone, LinkedIn is about building business relationships. It's more about connections than advertising.

YouTube. As most people already know, YouTube is all about videos. People post, and the world watches. You can send requests asking people to subscribe to your "channel," which is the place where you group the videos that you make and upload. As with any other social media site, you need to keep adding new material to keep your followers interested. There is a place for people to comment and an easy way to reply. In addition to posting videos of you reading your book or doing a classroom presentation, this is a good place to showcase book trailers. You can also post a link to your website, where followers can learn more about you and your book and, hopefully, make a purchase.

Pinterest. Pinterest allows users to share content through images and videos. There are brief descriptions to go with the posts, but the main focus of the site is visual. When users see something they like, they "pin it" to their "board." Other people can "repin" it to one of their own boards. If you are a writer and you create a Pinterest board titled "Fairy Books" that features your favorite books and writing tips, this board will attract other people who are also interested in fairy books. You can promote your board by linking and connecting to people who share the same style, or by pinning images that inspire your work. Promoting your own items, however, is less common than on other networking sites.

Goodreads. Goodreads is all about books. It's a place where readers gather, and there is an author program that can help you reach them. You can create a profile, add friends, join discussion groups and share your list of favorite books with your fans. You can also showcase your new releases and advertise your book signings. In addition, Goodreads sponsors book giveaways: You insert the information, and your giveaway will be posted on the dates you choose. When the giveaway offer ends, Goodreads will select the winner and send you the winner's name and contact information so you can then send them a book. In the meantime, hundreds of people have seen the name and summary of your book.

IBPA. The Independent Book Publishers Association has initiated an exciting social media site of its own—exciting because it's a place where you can interact and share ideas with other authors and independent publishers. Run by professionals in the book industry, it provides an excellent networking venue. You can post multiple photos, ask questions and share articles with ease. In addition, the site posts information about the latest news in the book community, and provides numerous groups and discussion forums. (You can read more about IBPA in the section titled "Writers Associations.")

Benefits of Using Social Media

No matter which methods or platforms you choose, there are certain marketing benefits most of them provide:

They are relatively easy to use. You can actually sit by the computer in your pajamas and sip your coffee while sending information about your book all over the world. I'm not belittling the amount of time that still goes into planning, organizing and posting, but how else can you reach so many people in such a short period of time?

Your audience awaits you. Turn on your computer, post a video or send out a tweet, and people are there to receive it. You have the ability to reach hundreds, maybe thousands of people at one time. This is truly incredible! One of the beauties of social media is that it centers around interaction with potential customers, and so many of them are right out there, ready to receive your information.

Shares will generate shares. You can create exponential growth when you share information with someone who then shares the information with others, and so on… The added beauty of this process is that it can all be accomplished quickly and easily, and again, in your pajamas!

Swapping knowledge is a benefit. It's not just about selling your book. Social media provides an easy way to help others and learn from them in return. The knowledge and sharing goes both ways. When I was working on this book, I asked my Facebook friends what questions or comments about self-publishing they would like to see addressed. I'm happy to include their ideas, along with my answers that I hope will help them.

Good things can happen. We have all seen the fabulous success stories started by a post going viral on the Internet. This is one virus you would welcome into your life!

Which Ones Should You Choose?

As you can see, each of these networking platforms has its own methods and character. Each reaches a very large audience. And there are others that I haven't mentioned. No one can tell you which arena is best for you, but you can experiment with the ones you like and see how they work and how they feel to you. Whatever you decide to do, you need to realize that social media marketing takes time; it's not an overnight event. It works best when used in conjunction with traditional marketing methods.

As with any marketing program, you are not the only one who sometimes feels like you are spinning wheels in sand. The efforts are cumulative, and seeing results often takes time. So be patient, and don't beat yourself up. Stay with it, and you will eventually reap the benefits!

Basic Guidelines and Social Media Etiquette

Whichever one, or ones, you choose, here are a few suggestions to help guide you:

Fill out your profile completely. People want to know who you really are, and they want to know what you do. If you are promoting yourself as an author and offering writing tips, people want to know your credentials. In addition, if you would like to network with people in your community, or invite people to your book events, be sure you include your location in your profile.

Put up a photo of yourself. Many people (me included) will not want to "associate" with you online if you don't show your face. People are more likely to want to engage with a real person than a generic silhouette.

Don't talk incessantly about yourself and your book. Don't make every post or tweet or photo an advertisement. Don't inundate your friends with posts about your book. Do comment on their posts, tweets and photos. Share ideas, offer advice and ask questions. Be a friend; share photos of your family and pets. All this can be done in addition to sharing information about your book and the events you are planning. Remember that, just as quickly as you were followed, you will be unfollowed if your content is deemed unimportant, annoying or boring.

Post photos. It's much more interesting to look at a photo than a block of text. People who are in a hurry and are scanning through their posts are more likely to stop to look at an eye-catching photo than a bunch of words. Post photos of yourself at a book signing, or of one of the new illustrations for your book, or even a photo of your book displayed on a bookstore shelf.

Post one or two photos at a time. As much as people like to look at photos, they are not always anxious to scroll through ten or twelve pictures of your last book event, or any other topic for that matter. Share your pictures throughout many posts. This gives you more exposure and keeps people from skipping over the entire lot.

Ask for opinions. Numerous times I have seen authors post photos of several possible book covers and ask for opinions on which one to choose. I actually did that with the cover of this book, and received extremely helpful suggestions. People love to weigh in and help. Going back to my idea about the importance of focus groups, what larger focus group could you possibly ask for? Just be sure to write back. Let your followers know you are paying attention and that you appreciate their input.

Respond to people. No one likes a one-way friendship. Be courteous, and pay attention to what your networking friends are sharing or promoting.

Provide a link to Your website. If you don't have a website, at least provide a link to wherever your book is sold. There's no point in promoting a book that no one can purchase.

And now, about that website…

Traffic to My Website Before and After a Facebook Ad

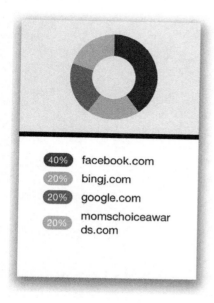

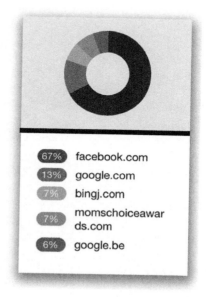

42. Do You Need a Website?

In today's world of social media, do you still need your own website? Don't answer that question until you finish reading this section. Let's take a look at some of the advantages of having your own website:

It provides information about you and your book. Whether prospective buyers arrive at your website via social media or as an outcome of your in-person promotions, they can find a lot more information and photos when they get there. You will be able to provide many more words and pictures on your site than you can cram into your posts or talk about at book signings. You can also make this process work in reverse: You can post links on your website that direct visitors to your social media pages.

It can make a great first impression. An attractive, professional-looking website provides a terrific introduction to your book. If customers are surfing the web to find children's books, you want them to stop, take a look at your site, and say "Wow!"

It's a professional business tool. One of the first questions you will be asked by potential customers, teachers and event planners is, "Do you have a website?" Saying "yes" adds a higher level of credibility to your business. It projects more professionalism than saying, "No, but you can follow me on Twitter."

Other authors have websites. All the more reason for you to have one, too. If customers are searching online for rhyming books, for example, they will look for the websites that feature these books. If you fit this category but don't have a website, that would leave you out of the picture.

Where else will people go? When you hand out postcards and bookmarks to promote your book, but you don't have a website, what will you say to drive people to get more information? Please like my Facebook page? Have you seen my new Pinterest posts? You get my point.

Millions of people shop on the Internet. Actually, millions and millions of people rely on the Internet when they to do their shopping. Customers can't find you if you aren't there.

You can make quick updates. Think of your website as your online brochure. It is much easier and quicker to update information about your books on your website than to have brochures and flyers constantly reprinted. A new book or event can be posted on your website in a matter of minutes.

Your store is never closed. Unlike a brick-and-mortar store, your website is a store that stays open 24 hours a day, 7 days a week. Customers can place orders any time of day or night, even from other countries or time zones. It's essential to either sell your book directly from your website or provide a link with a large, highly visible button that takes the customers directly to where they can purchase the book.

PayPal is one of the easiest methods for accepting payments through your website; they provide everything you need, including a "shopping cart." Your customers are able to pay by credit card or check, and many of your customers will already have a PayPal account. PayPal is a trusted name in business, and using the option may also add a bit of credibility to your site. The setup information is relatively easy to follow, and there are even live people in the customer support department who are available for help.

It can provide fun. Yes, you can make your website a fun place for children to visit, as well as adults. You can provide links to your video trailers, have a page where you post letters, drawings or photos of your fans, and post coloring pages that can be easily downloaded and printed.

Choosing a Hosting Company

Now that you've seen the many advantages of having a website, you can look online for lists of web hosting companies, and compare their costs and services. Even if you have never thought of yourself as technologically inclined, you may surprise yourself. Many hosting companies include a free website builder. Most of these programs are easy to use, come with a ton of templates, and allow you to build and edit your site with just a few mouse clicks. (I was completely amazed at myself when I built my entire website in 3 days, and only cried once!)

One more bit of advice: Create a website that is a worthy representation of you and your books. Look at other authors' websites to help you decide which features you like. Make your site colorful, fun and easy to navigate.

How to Choose a Domain Name

Before you build your website, you will need to register a domain name. Choosing this name requires a lot of thought; don't just slap any old name on your website.

Make your domain name an easy-to-remember name that reflects your company or book titles. You don't want a name that is obscure, difficult to remember or has nothing to do with your books. The goal is for your name to match your brand. Make it cute, funny or catchy so it will be memorable. If you choose a name that is too generic, such as "cutechildrensbooks.com," Google will pull up every children's book on the market and no one will ever find you. You want a unique name that uses keywords for which people will likely be searching. For example, if you are planning to write a series of books about dragons, make sure your domain name has the word "dragon" in it, such as "dragonfarts.com." (See the section titled "Know The Importance of Keywords and SEO.")

Some authors use just their own name for their company and domain. However, if you wish to be taken seriously as a publisher, it definitely looks more professional to present yourself as a legitimate business, and naming your company is a step in the right direction. As soon as you have decided on your company name, register it right away as your domain name. The very day I named my company "Best Fairy Books" I registered the name "bestfairybooks.com". This was way before I had even finished writing my first book. I didn't want to take the chance that someone, somewhere, might also be thinking their fairy books were best.

One more tip: Make your domain name concise and to the point, avoiding numbers and hyphens if possible.

43. Know the Importance of Keywords and SEO

You have probably heard the term "search engine optimization" (SEO), but do you know what it means? In simple terms, it is a way to be found online. It involves choosing the words that best relate to the content on your website, blog and other web pages, and using them to attract more search engine traffic. The ultimate goal is to drive more people to wherever your book is sold. Some marketing companies specialize in SEO, however this can be a very costly project. If you choose to go that route, be sure to do your research before choosing a company to work with.

The correct use of keywords and SEO can lead to increased book sales. Here are some questions and answers that I believe will give you a better understanding of how it works:

How will prospective customers find you? Ask yourself the following questions: When customers are looking for a book with a topic similar to yours, what words will they type into a search engine like Google, Yahoo, or Bing that will enable your website or blog to show up? What words or phrases describe the content of your book? These are your keywords.

How do you choose your keywords? There are online sites where you can pay to have a search done for you, or you can do the work yourself. Think of the key words that describe your book. For example, some of *my* most frequently used keywords, ones that appear in almost everything I post are: *fairy book, rhyming book, preschool book, fantasy book, fairy tale, beginning reader, knot fairy, sock fairy, belly button fairy, fart fairy and freckle fairy.* These words relate to what my books are about. I wouldn't expect words like *author, publisher* or *children's books* to find me in the vast sea of other authors, publishers and children's books; these words are far too broad and used by too many other people. When I recently Googled *children's picture books,* I was offered a choice of 70,700,000 entries. This is why you need to be specific when choosing your keywords.

As you can see, a keyword is often a combination of words. If someone were to simply type in the word *knot*, for example, there's no telling how many thousands of listings would pop up. But type in *knot fairy,* and there I am.

How will the search engines find your keywords? Once you have identified your keywords and feel certain these are the words people are searching for, you need to use these important words in the main title and other headings of your website, blog, online press release and other information you publish on the Internet. It's actually a smart marketing strategy to think of your keywords *before* or *during* your website building so you can integrate them into the content of the site. The search engines will pick up the words and give the customers what they are looking for.

How do you use your keywords? When writing a post, blog or article, use as many of your keywords in the title as possible; a goal of 5 keywords is a good start. Be sure the title is readable, makes sense, is free of spelling errors and contains your primary keywords. An example of a catchy blog title might be: "Funny Fairy Books With Freckles and Farts." This would incorporate two of my book titles and add a bit of alliteration and humor. I actually Googled this imaginary title, and my books came up first on the list. If you can make your title fun and catchy, it will likely attract people's attention, even if it ends up appearing a little further down on the list. Be careful not to make your titles too long. My experience has been that Google will display between 63 and 69 characters (depending on your word breaks) and then truncate the title, resulting in some missing words, and perhaps words such as "and the..." now becoming the end of your title.

Remember:
Search engines can only give the customers what they are looking for if you put it out there for them.

44. The Many Layers of Marketing: Tie it All Together

When you plan your marketing campaign, you need to consider how you are going to allocate your time and money. You may think it's a good idea to do one thing at a time, but that may prove to be counterproductive. The more you can layer at once, especially as you launch your book, the greater the impact will be. Let's say you are planning your launch party. You advertise it on several social media sites simultaneously, while at the same time your press release is hitting the newspapers, your sell sheets are in the hands of bookstore managers, and you have several blog interviews underway. The resulting coverage is exponentially larger than if you tackled these promotions one at a time. The key in this situation is to think ahead and work on becoming efficient in managing your time. It will certainly prove to be time well spent.

Piggyback Your Events

Piggybacking is a way to leverage your marketing dollars by layering marketing strategies and tying events together. This system of careful planning has enabled me not only to save money while attending out-of-town book signings, conferences and festivals, but also to earn it. Here's an example of how it works: If you are going to be exhibiting at a Saturday book fair in an area that requires an overnight stay, scheduling is the key. First, if the event is on Saturday, I usually plan to go early on Friday, leaving me time to schedule either an afternoon school visit or an evening library visit, thus making Friday a profitable day. I also do my best to find some type of event to squeeze into Sunday before heading home. Some of the Sunday events I have successfully arranged include an early signing at a bookstore, a grandparents' club brunch at a local church, and a presentation for a Brownie troop. Check the online newspapers for the town you are planning to visit, and be creative. You will come home thoroughly exhausted and totally happy.

Say Yes to Every Opportunity

Throughout the book I have mentioned numerous possibilities to explore for signings and presentations. I strongly recommend, at least in the beginning, that you never say no to an opportunity to share your books. Notice that I said "share" your books; I didn't say "sell" your books. Not every venue will result in sales. But if you think of every opportunity as a place to sow some seeds, you will be amazed at what you will reap. I have received calls months, even years, after events that I had thought of as worthless. Even if the event turns out to be what you consider a dud, if no one buys a book, or if you are asked to do the presentation for free, be gracious, smile, share your books and give everyone a bookmark. One of the strangest requests I have had was from a pediatrician who wanted to have a book signing at his office on a Saturday morning and invite his patients to attend. I said yes. I only sold a few books, but I spread a lot of good will in my town, and later sold additional books to some of the attendees at a bookstore signing event. And that's not all; every time I have an event, he offers to place flyers and postcards in his waiting room.

Always Ask for Referrals

Wherever you go, ask for referrals. After doing a school presentation, I always say something like this to the teacher: "Thank you for inviting me into your classroom. It was a delightful experience. Do you know other teachers who would be happy to have an author visit their classroom?" Sometimes teachers say they will be glad to pass my information along; other times they give me names of people to contact.

Advertise Where You Have Been and What You Have Done

As you arrange events, you can add them to your brochures and website, and brag about them on your social media sites. Do the same with photos: Take your camera wherever you go and share your experiences wherever you can. It's easy to create a collage featuring photos of you at various events. Turn the collage into flyers for use as promotional tools, either on social media or to show prospective schools or event organizers.

There's an expression, "If you throw enough mud on the wall, some of it is bound to stick." Think of every place you visit as another mile traveled on this exciting journey and more mud on the wall. Just keep throwing!

45. Translating Marketing Into $$$: Following the Money Trail

Throughout this book I have been careful not to mention my exact costs. My reasoning was based on the huge variation in the cost of each venue and service. As my wonderful friends and beta readers read my manuscript, they all asked me the same questions: "Where did you make the most money?" and "What worked best for you?" Developing my answers turned out to be a worthwhile exercise for me. I took a long, hard look at my past efforts—and my ledger pages. It's important to note that what gave me the most pleasure also brought in the most money. Is that a coincidence? For me, the path to success has been paved with people. Whether at schools, libraries, book fairs or chance encounters, the bulk of my books have been sold directly to customers.

I am by no means discounting the lucrative sales made by my hard-working distributor; but many self-publishers are not working with distributors and I want them to recognize the potentially profitable avenues open to them. Ask yourself these questions: How much time do I have? What will my budget allow? What will I enjoy the most? What am I willing to do even if I don't enjoy it? What am I not willing to do? What will sell the most books?

With the many new social media forums available today, you may find other marketing methods that work better for you. The choice is yours—and there are so many options to consider; however, I will share with you the money trail that has worked for me:

To Begin With

I did my best to produce a top-notch book. I know I keep repeating this, but my wise school principal husband always tells me you have to say something at least seven times before someone really "gets it." You *must* produce an exceptional book if you want exceptional sales. I'll say it another way: A boring book will produce a boring sales record. In addition, producing books that are timely, relevant and appealing to a large percentage of young readers is another important part of the equation. How did I know my books would sell? You should know the answer by now: They were loved and approved by my focus groups, and they were professionally illustrated, edited, designed and printed—a winning combination.

I ordered the largest quantity of books I could comfortably afford. This is where being a bit gutsy came into play. The cost to print my picture books in hardcover format, with a dust jacket and CD, was quoted at approximately $6 per book for 1000 books vs. $3 per book if I ordered 5000 books. I chose the latter option. When I sell each of my books for the retail price of $16.95, my profit is $13.95. Even with the discounts I offer, and costs associated with each venue, this is a nice profit margin.

I sought reviews and awards. Simply put, reviews and awards can lead to more sales, yielding more income. People like to see what you've accomplished, and both reviews and awards can say a lot. You can brag all day about your book on Facebook and Twitter, but displaying a book with an award sticker or some glowing reviews from reputable reviewers speaks directly about the quality of your book.

My Retail Markets

I am always on the lookout for retail outlets for my books. My most profitable ones have been consistent:

School Visits. A day spent in a school can be extremely lucrative. I charge $400 for a school visit. This includes three presentations in a day, with 45 children in each group, yielding the potential to sell 75 to 100 books—at retail. If I do one school visit a week, there's a good chance for me to sell 300 books in a month. I then use the information and photos from the visits as posts on social media sites, often resulting in more sales through Amazon and my website.

Book Fairs and Other Festivals. A day spent at a book fair, or any other large venue, can put your smiling face and shiny new book in front of hundreds—even thousands—of people. At each book festival, gift fair and holiday bazaar, my goal is to sell 100 books. Often I meet my goal; sometimes I don't. Either way, I am happy if several hundred people looked at my books and went home with a bookmark or other marketing item containing my website address and pictures of my books. Even if I sell fewer books than I had hoped, these are still retail sales. I go to as many book fairs and other festivals as I can. As I mentioned earlier, face-to-face sales are my favorite—and most lucrative—sales venue.

Wholesale and Niche Markets

Gift shops, etc. If you follow my advice and make your book attractive and appealing, it may fit nicely into the category of "gift items." I have been able to gain a number of privately owned gift shops as customers. Each store usually orders an average of twelve to eighteen books a month. Most of the owners have asked for a 45% to 50% discount; my books that retail for $16.95 cost them approximately $8.50, allowing me a profit of about $5.50 per book.

Distributor. Having a distributor, I receive a check twice a year for the books they have sold to bookstores and libraries. This number fluctuates, and often reflects my own promotional efforts. I let my distributor know where I will be and when, so they can contact their clients in the area. With the distributor's discount, I receive approximately $8 for each book they sell. (Remember: Net sales equals retail price minus account discount, which is usually around 50 percent.) I still make $5 profit on each book, which is still a profit and is better than having the books sit around collecting dust.

Internet Market and Other Arenas

It's difficult for me to determine with complete accuracy the number or origin of my internet sales. Some of these sales go through my distributor, while others come to my website. I have asked customers how they found out about my books, and many have said they saw them at a festival, then saw them again on Amazon or Facebook. Or they say they met me somewhere, but not sure exactly where, and they had picked up a bookmark and later checked out my website. This is why I stress the use of a variety of marketing venues, along with piggybacking events.

When I spend more time on internet marketing, such as Facebook ad campaigns featuring sale prices, or free e-books on Amazon, my sales peak; it takes a lot of advertising to keep those sales up. What I *have* been able to ascertain from internet sales is that, for me, they are not nearly as lucrative as my in-person sales.

Where Do Book Signings Fit In?

You may have noticed that I haven't mentioned book signings among my important sales. Unfortunately, unless you are a *very big* star in the world of books, signings are a hit-and-miss source of income. Other than my book launch parties, which typically draw several hundred little fairy followers, my other book signings have been variable. Even with bookstore sales rising after each signing, this is not an income that I have been able to count on as being consistent.

Keep in Mind

Markup is a major factor. Selling your books at retail is lucrative, but *only* if your printing cost allows you to realize a profit. I am definitely not recommending that you stock your garage with books. Do only what your budget allows. My goal in sharing this information is to help you make informed decisions.

A Few More Tips That Might Help

If your book is successful, follow up with another equally wonderful book. When I produced my second and third books, I noticed an interesting phenomenon: When customers liked my books, they often said, "I'll take one of each." My pricing policy helped, as I offer a discount for multiple books. You will most likely develop a following at events, especially if you exhibit at the same ones each year; people will be watching for your next book. Just make sure your new book is equally wonderful. Don't make the mistake of just slapping another book together quickly so you can sell more books. Take the same care and go through the same steps as with your first book.

Share Experiences on Social Media. For effective social media marketing, I try not to post something if I have nothing worthwhile to say. How many times can you post "Buy My Book" before people block your posts? Share your experiences instead. People will stop scrolling to look at your photos if you are surrounded by classroom children, or have a line of people at your booth, or have the familiar Barnes & Noble background behind you. What I have done is: Go to an event, win an award or get a review, and then blog, share and post about it. My goal is to make sales, then drive customers to Amazon or my website in order to make more sales. I do this again…and again…and again…

Other marketing opportunities have come my way and I have taken advantage of many of them. There is often no way to track the sales that come from promotions such as press releases, mass mailings, postcard campaigns or other similar endeavors.

No matter how much marketing you plan to do, you MUST first produce a captivating book, free of grammatical errors, with a cover that reaches out and grabs you and a story that begs to be read over and over again.

46. Going Forth: Keep Writing it Right!

Your book is finished and the rest of your life has begun. From now on you are an author! But before you get carried away with pride, there's something very important to consider, something that possibly no one has ever told you: *You must always write it right!*

If you have taken my advice, your book has been professionally edited; the spelling is perfect, the punctuation in place. But, who will edit the multitude of forms and letters you will be called upon as an author to write as you move on? There will be letters to schools, libraries and bookstores. There will be bios to write for applications to book fairs and other festivals. There will be press releases and sell sheets to create. There will be postcards, bookmarks, brochures, flyers and pricing signs.

Let's not forget emails. They are so important that they need a paragraph of their own; emails have become an accepted method of communication. They are quick and easy to send and, for that very reason, have a tendency to be brief and sloppy. We have all received emails that consist of one long, run-on sentence with no punctuation; however, emails can be extremely important, and therefore also deserve correct grammar and punctuation. Stop and think before you hit the "send" button. Take a minute to reread and make corrections.

Your website and social media presence are also a representation of you and your writing skills. Check and double-check your website for coherency, grammar and punctuation. If you send an email request to a blogger asking for a review of your book, and your email is riddled with mistakes, you are sending a negative message about your writing ability. When I read poorly written Facebook posts in which authors are describing their books, would I purchase their books? Absolutely not.

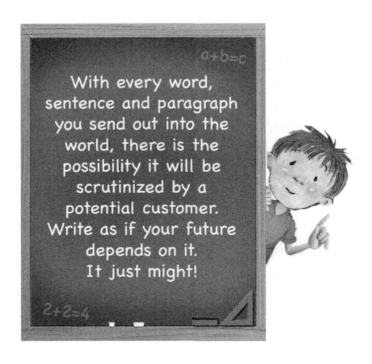

With every word, sentence and paragraph you send out into the world, there is the possibility it will be scrutinized by a potential customer. Write as if your future depends on it. It just might!

A FEW LAST WORDS

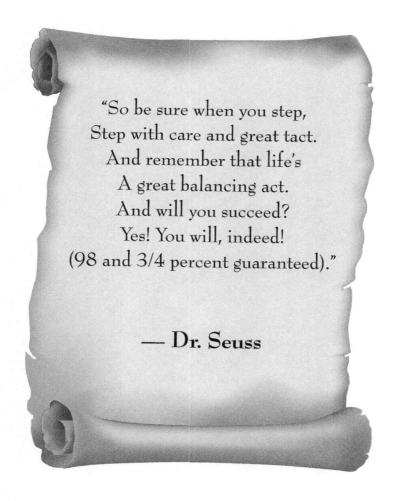

"So be sure when you step,
Step with care and great tact.
And remember that life's
A great balancing act.
And will you succeed?
Yes! You will, indeed!
(98 and 3/4 percent guaranteed)."

— Dr. Seuss

47. The End is Just the Beginning

How do I end this book, when the end is really the beginning? I've pondered this for quite a while and have decided to end by sharing my deepest thoughts. Here goes: Writing a book is like having a baby!

Really. It's true. I've experienced both, so I should know. (Unlike my husband, who has never had a baby, yet claims that his kidney stone was much worse than childbirth.) But I digress. As an author, I've worked on each of my books for many months, or even many, many months. Each project, like an unborn child, slowly grew and developed. All the while, my eyes remained on the future, wondering what it held for me and my new "little one." Eventually, after what seemed like an eternity, the labor began. The final stages of tying the book together, working with the editor, deliberating over the illustrations, and making many last-minute adjustments were often intensely laborious.

Then one day, just when I felt I couldn't wait any longer, the book finally arrived. So exciting! I clasped the new book in my arms and held it to my heart. Each new book, just like a new baby, seems so familiar, yet at the same time, there is the nagging feeling that I've never seen it before. I know that deep down I love it because it is all mine, yet I really don't know it at all.

And just like having a baby, this is only the beginning, the first step in a very long parent-child relationship. So much depends on how I "raise" this baby. If I nurture it by scheduling promotions, marketing well, and putting my heart and soul into the little newcomer, I will be a very proud parent indeed. And if I am lucky, I will forget the short-lived pain and suffering, and do it all over again.

Acknowledgements

I have learned that just because it's called "self-publishing" doesn't mean you should try to do it all yourself. This book is about people—the people who believed in me, took this journey with me and helped me along the way. Writing may at times be a lonely trade; self-publishing, on the other hand, is a team effort. I have met so many people in the process—too many to name, but I will always be grateful to each and every one of them. I can't imagine trying to *self*-publish all by *myself*.

I want to send a heartfelt, special thank you to:

Dr. Seuss, in his special library in heaven, whose books taught me at a young age to think in rhyme.

Kristi Bridgeman,* an illustrator's illustrator, for showing me the workings of her truly creative mind and teaching me to find the perfect balance between words and pictures.

Jeff Urbancic,** my graphic designer extraordinaire, for designing this book, for the beautiful magic he performed on my children's books and for always smiling when I ask him to make "just one more teensy change."

Carol Wise,*** my outstanding editor, for helping me get my message across in just the right amount of words.

Judy Croiter, my friend and first proofreader, for putting up with my extra commas and overused "howevers."

Lois Petren, my astute beta reader, for a thorough job, adding a little more work and a lot of ideas to this book.

Bob Hartenstine, a fellow writer and friend indeed, who was always willing to lend an educated pair of eyes.

Aziz and Rizwan at Amica, Inc., for printing top-quality children's books that made it possible for me to reach so many young readers.

My focus group - Emily, Lindsay, Justin, Kaitlyn, Jordan, Katya, Max, Leah, Connor, and anyone else they could drag in to listen to my stories, offer their wonderful ideas, and be so brutally honest.

Cindy Melrose at Barnes & Noble in Bel Air, Maryland, for believing that together we could draw 300 people to our book signings.

My daughter, Traci, and my son, Mike, for always encouraging me and being there to support me. After telling you for so many years that *you* can do anything, thanks for believing that I could, too.

My husband, business partner and best friend, Harry, the perfect mix of bully and teddy bear, for always being there, even when the odds seemed overwhelming. I'm so happy I created you!

My precious grandchildren, the creators and designers of my journey. I love you to the moon and back—and more!

*Kristi Bridgeman resides on Vancouver Island, B.C., Canada. Known for her sepia tones and glowing lines, some of her work has been said to resemble that of Victorian children's illustrators. She has illustrated numerous children's books, has won many awards for her illustrations, and has been honored as one of the 150 Top Women Artists through the Federation of Canadian Artists. Her work can be seen at: www.kristibridgeman.com.

**Jeff Urbancic has a Bachelor of Fine Arts degree in Communications Arts. He is an accomplished art director and graphic designer. He has designed books covering a variety of subjects; however, he gains the most enjoyment out of designing children's books. Jeff lives in Virginia with his wife and two children. He can be contacted through The Urbancic Creative Group, LLC at: jurbancic5@comcast.net.

***Carol Wise is a trained linguist. Having retired from the academic world and adopted a productive life of editing, she resides in happy obscurity with her husband, son, dogs, and lizard. You can find her company, Writes of Passage, LLC, on Upwork.com.

About the Author

Bobbie Hinman's five children's picture books, *The Knot Fairy, The Sock Fairy, The Belly Button Fairy, The Fart Fairy* and *The Freckle Fairy* have received a combined total of twenty-five children's book awards.

Bobbie has been a speaker and presenter at numerous schools, libraries and bookstores, as well as major book festivals and fairy festivals all across the United States and in Canada. Her articles have appeared in the Independent Book Publishers Association magazine and in many blogs and interviews. Bobbie's bookstore events have been featured in the *Barnes & Noble Inside* newsletter.

Growing up in Baltimore, Maryland, Bobbie graduated from Towson University with a B.S. degree in Elementary Education and a minor in Children's Literature. As an elementary teacher, she kept abreast of the world of children's books, always encouraging reading as a path to a successful future. She always knew deep down that someday she would write a children's book.

After having children, Bobbie and her husband decided to move to a farm and follow a healthy lifestyle. She gave up teaching and devoted the next decade to raising children, golden retrievers, horses, cats and a goat named Timothy. An advocate of healthy eating, Bobbie went on to author and co-author seven successful cookbooks. It wouldn't be long before she was "back in the game," deeply involved in the world of children's literature.

Bobbie and her husband, Harry, live in Florida with their two kitties, Twinkle and Boo. The book business keeps them very busy. When asked if she is now retired, Bobbie often answers with, "no, just tired." Their children are grown, and the Hinmans are the proud grandparents of thirteen grandchildren, who have played a significant role in the development of the Fairy Book Series.

Index

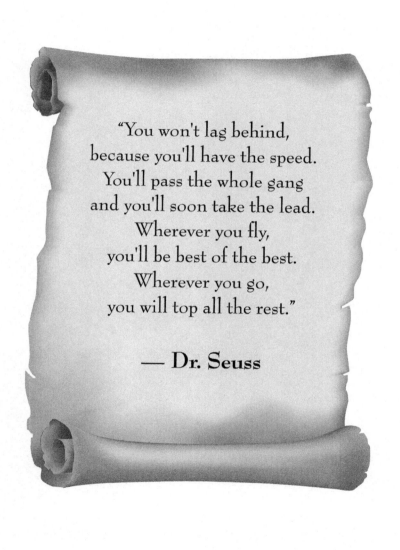

"You won't lag behind,
because you'll have the speed.
You'll pass the whole gang
and you'll soon take the lead.
Wherever you fly,
you'll be best of the best.
Wherever you go,
you will top all the rest."

— Dr. Seuss

Printed in Great Britain
by Amazon

26808030R00163